Poetry Ireland Review 126

Eagarthóir / Editor
EAVAN BOLAND

© Poetry Ireland Ltd 2018

Poetry Ireland Ltd/Éigse Éireann Teo gratefully acknowledges the assistance of
The Arts Council/An Chomhairle Ealaíon and The Arts Council of Northern Ireland.

AMBITIOUS PLANS NEED EXTRAORDINARY SUPPORTERS
Your support will help connect more people to poetry through our performance, writer development, education, and publishing programmes. We are particularly keen to build relationships with partners who wish to join us in making the Poetry Ireland Centre a reality at 11 Parnell Square East, D1. Find out how at www.poetryireland.ie/support

FOUNDING PARTNERS
Adrian Brinkerhoff Poetry Fund of the Sidney E Frank Foundation

POETRY PATRONS: EPIC
Thomas Dillon Redshaw

POETRY PATRONS: LYRIC
Eithne Hand, Ruth Webster

POETRY PATRONS: SONNET
Neville Keery, Nana Lampton, William McConkey, Joan and Joe McBreen, Anonymous

POETRY PATRON: HAIKU
Ciara McCluskey

FRIENDS OF POETRY IRELAND
Desmond Windle, Rachel Joynt, Noel and Anne Monahan, Maurice Earls, Mary Shine Thompson, Seán Coyle, Andrew Caldicott, Henry and Deirdre Comerford, Maura Hanlon

Poetry Ireland Review is published three times a year by Poetry Ireland. The Editor enjoys complete autonomy in the choice of material published. The contents of this publication should not be taken to reflect either the views or the policy of the publishers.

ISBN: 978-1-902121-74-1   ISSN: 0332-2998

PUBLICATIONS TEAM: **Paul Lenehan** and **Rachel Botha**, with the assistance of
Andi Grene, **Chase Wilmot**, and **Orla Higgins**

IRISH-LANGUAGE EDITOR: **Caitlín Nic Íomhair**
DESIGN: **Alistair Keady** (www.hexhibit.com)
COVER CREDIT: from *Beginning of Darkness* (2016) by **Martin Gale**

Contents
Poetry Ireland Review 126

Eavan Boland	5	EDITORIAL
Abayomi Animashaun	7	WHEN LIGHTS GO OUT IN THE VILLAGE
Anthony Caleshu	8	THE CREATURELY AMONGST US ARE CELEBRATING THE ADVENT OF A VANQUISHED SPECIES
Enda Coyle-Greene	9	ANGEL FROM MONTGOMERY
Roderic Vincent	10	POEM ON A RAINY BIRTHDAY
Raine Geoghegan	12	THE GREENHOUSE
Louise C Callaghan	14	MURMURATION OF STARLINGS
Rosie Lavan	15	REVIEW: MARTINA EVANS, MARIA MCMANUS
Jenny Carla Moran	20	I LIVE IN THE VANISHING TRIANGLE
Greg Delanty	22	MONARCH BUTTERFLY
Janet Sutherland	23	DILAPIDATIONS I
Lucia Kenny	24	ROOTS
Milena Williamson	25	THE OUTING
John Greening	26	HYPERION'S SONG OF DESTINY
John Noonan	27	HYMN OF INNOCENCE
Nicholas Grene	28	REVIEW: DEREK MAHON, PETER FALLON
Marie Morrin	34	GODMOTHER
Terry Doyle	36	GARDENING IN MUTE
Colin Pink	37	HOPEFULLY TO DWELL
Ali Lewis	38	LOVE POEM TO YOUR SELF-SUFFICIENCY
Gerard Smyth	39	IDOLATRY
Phil Kirby	40	LANDSCAPE/PORTRAIT
Lottie Limb	41	ESSAY: BLANAID SALKELD
Rachel Coventry	47	ALL METAPHORS ARE FLAWED
Michael Dooley	48	SOLSTICE
Orla Fay	49	POET IN A TRAIN STATION BAR
Mary O'Donnell	50	DOORWAYS
Niamh Nic Ghabhann	52	REVIEW: COLM KEEGAN, ELAINE FEENEY, DENISE BLAKE
Maria Isakova-Bennett	57	BREGDAN
Medbh McGuckian	58	RESPONSES TO WEATHERING
Mary Finn	60	ON SAMOS
Thomas O'Grady	61	ENVOI
Cecilia McGovern	62	CROSSOVERS
Mary Shine Thompson	63	REVIEW: THEO DORGAN, MATTHEW SWEENEY, EVA BOURKE
Mary Wilkinson	67	STROKE
Ruth Esther Gilmore	68	OYSTERCATCHERS
Jo Burns	69	AS THE SAYING GOES, IT GOES TOO FAST
Justin Quinn	70	IVANA LOMOVÁ'S NEOREALIST PORTRAIT OF A COUPLE
Christian Wethered	71	PRESENT

Thomas McCarthy	72	REVIEW: MEDBH MCGUCKIAN, JOHN F DEANE, JAMES HARPUR
Christina Lloyd	76	AT MACY'S
Deborah Moffatt	77	A NIGHT AT THE AVEROF
Mairéad Donnellan	78	EXHORTATION
Liam Aungier	79	HEDGEHOGS
Nancy Anne Miller	80	MOSQUITO NET AT ELMA NAPIER'S ESTATE
Mary Kathryn Jablonski	81	HEARTSEASE
Kathryn Simmonds	82	NOVEMBER
Jessica Traynor	83	REVIEW: JAMES O'SULLIVAN, LIZ QUIRKE, COLIN DARDIS
Laurence O'Dwyer	87	MINKE WHALE
Elizabeth Scanlon	88	POST-POST-INTERNET
Colette Bryce	89	AN AMENDMENT
	90	UNTITLED, DUBLIN
	91	THE PIGEON
Annemarie Ní Churreáin	92	THE DEATH OF QUEEN SCOTIA
Helen Meany	93	REVIEW: TOM FRENCH, JOSEPH WOODS, LEANNE O'SULLIVAN
Anne Tannam	96	PICKING FIGS
John Fallon	97	OUTSIDE CALICO MACK'S
Simon Ó Faoláin	98	CÁNÓG DHUBH
John Smelcer	100	A LINGERING DOUBT
	100	THE DAY AFTER SATURDAY
	101	RAVENCOLOUR
Fióna Bolger	102	BE CAREFUL WHAT YOU WRITE
Nell Regan	103	ESSAY: THE POETRY OF MICHEÁL MAC LIAMMÓIR IN TRANSLATION
Richard Tillinghast	112	I TUNED UP SEÁN'S GUITAR
Eavan Boland	113	FEATURED POET: ROISIN KELLY
Roisin Kelly	115	IN AMERICA
	116	DOMÍNIO VALE DO MONDEGO
Maureen Boyle	117	REVIEW: KATE DEMPSEY, ELAINE COSGROVE, ALICE KINSELLA
Lex Runciman	121	NEWS, 1949
Billy Fenton	122	HEALER 2
Heidi Beck	123	AN ENDING WITH FOOD AND FLOWERS
Kathleen McCann	124	CROSSING TO ENGLAND FOR HARVEST WORK
Emer Lyons	125	CORK CITY, 1974
Paul Bregazzi	126	TALISMAN
Lorraine Carey	127	STARCHED SHIRTS
Bernard O'Donoghue	128	REVIEW: SEAMUS HEANEY
Mícheál McCann	131	HOOK-UP
Peter Wyton	132	FIRST DISOBEDIENCE
Yvonne Reddick	134	SPIKENARD
Stephen Knight	135	IN MY OTHER LIFE
Notes on Contributors	136	

Editorial

What does a poet look like? That question, which seems so out of place now, was once less so. Years ago poets' appearances were noted, their likenesses commented on in letters, novels, poems. Often the poet was the mirror of the moment. Or at least thought to be. 'I am of those weak women who reverence strong men', wrote Elizabeth Barrett Browning in a letter to a friend. A strange statement from this deeply independent poet, but not an unusual one in the Victorian era. 'The greatest men, whether poets or historians', wrote Ruskin, 'live entirely in their own age'.

In fact, for 150 years each society, each decade, seemed to dress a poet in its own hopes and concerns. In this context poets, almost exclusively male, were slightly less respectably costumed than the mainstream variant. For all that, their departures from the norm, their apparent freedoms, were on a short leash. The ages they lived in were leashed as well.

Then and later, appearances mattered. The American poet, Louise Bogan, who wrote poetry reviews for *The New Yorker*, commented on Yeats. 'William Butler Yeats', she wrote 'first appears, in the memories of his contemporaries, as a rarefied human being: a tall, dark-visaged young man who walked the streets of Dublin and London in a poetic hat, cloak, and flowing tie, intoning verses.' Appearances also seemed to denote the inner world as well as the outer one. 'Come to lunch', Virginia Woolf wrote to a friend. 'Eliot will be there in a four-piece suit.'

What does this mean? For the working poet, for the active reader? And was there anything wrong with describing what poets wore fifty years ago, how they looked, how they were observed? I think there was. Lying under those sentimental or sardonic comments, littered throughout novels, newspapers, letters, was a darker outline. A different query lay under the more obvious one. If asking what a poet looked like was one variant then another was a shadow-shape in the water, unspoken but related: Who didn't look like a poet?

In the last two centuries, that shadow question has had a difficult history. Women, minorities, communities on the margins of a society – at first none of them looked like poets. Therefore, the logic went, they couldn't be poets. None of them were included in the inventory of descriptions, word-portraits, commentaries on a poet's life in the world. To be poets they had to be approved. And they weren't.

Because poetry is associated with free expression, many people resist thinking a society could have the power to issue or withhold permissions about a poet's identity. That such permissions, or their denial, could be mediated through comments about appearance. But they could and they were.

One of the pleasures of editing *Poetry Ireland Review* – the same is true of the Stegner workshop at Stanford – is the chance to see close-up these categories disappearing, and just how little tolerance is left for them. There are no easy definitions now, no agreed cut-outs. Part of the reason is that the social consensus that underpinned those divisions has broken down. The woman in traffic, the man at the gym, the teenager seeming to limp along with a sporting injury, the trans writer, the hermetic one, the emerging writer of colour – any or all of them could be poets.

Maybe the larger reason for this is that poetry has grown tired of its own exclusions. New energies have come to the threshold of an old art. Clearly they should be welcomed. In Poetry Ireland they certainly have been. The democratic sparkle of spoken word platforms, the intensity of interdisciplinary collaborations where music and language meet, the power of performance, and the proper loneliness of the page – all of these are factors in our much wider sense today of who is a poet, who can be a poet, who looks like a poet. This may seem like a small thing. But small things in the arts can sometimes turn out to be saving graces. This may be one of them.

– Eavan Boland

Abayomi Animashaun

WHEN LIGHTS GO OUT IN THE VILLAGE

And the watchman,
Tired from patrols,
Leans on the gates,

I find myself awake
In the same dream

Of goats painting
Their hooves green.

Of women, drunk
On the aroma
Of bell-peppers,

Passed out
In the village square
Naked.

Of my father again
In the family shrine

Crossing himself
Then reciting

Bismillah

Hoping the floating boat
That ferries the dead
Passes by

Without dropping anchor
Outside my house.

Anthony Caleshu

THE CREATURELY AMONGST US ARE CELEBRATING THE ADVENT OF A VANQUISHED SPECIES

The creaturely amongst us are celebrating the advent of a vanquished species. It takes the fallen to know the fallen, say the fallen. In the desert, or alone at sea, all living things know no word can overcome another word – not *belief*, neither *doubt*. Our confessions about loneliness and congregation are the stuff of devotion: who sent me here (this island)? who called me here (the sky)? we ask ourselves daily. If there's a God within us, there's a god outside us: equal and opposite, and so on, and so on. We wander and return, getting lost in the spirit world, now rent but thick with so many of our kind. We reconstitute the wilderness within us constantly. From the backs of our throats, pooling up from the lungs, we sweat abjection until spontaneous-combustion. We make our way by the light in our bodies: shining out of every eye, every pore.

Enda Coyle-Greene

ANGEL FROM MONTGOMERY

Uneasy suddenly, driving home
too soon, what could I know
that music will not soothe –
what makes me choose to sing
a prayer not meant but still sent
a cappella to pin wings
on to an angel set for flight?

Tall trees stand sentinel all the way
to the Cross. Tonight goes by
already scored by absences,
no orchestras, no choirs,
inside two hours
my mother will have died.

Roderic Vincent

POEM ON A RAINY BIRTHDAY
  – for Jess

Her smaller hand holds
the hand that holds
the umbrella. It's wetter
out there, and in here
things might get romantic.
A roof over our heads,
the homely chat of rain
on a tent. But this is what
we cannot do together:
there isn't room under
this canopy. We could be
huddled from the world,
but we fight over the handle,
hand over fist, the flag
of victory wobbling above.
She calls me selfish when
I only want to protect
and provide full coverage
for her. I'm skirting the over-
hang of trees, steering her
round a lamppost. Above all
I want to avoid a clash
with oncoming umbrellas.
I give no thought to the equal
distribution of territory.
She offers to withdraw
the little floral fold-out
brolly from her handbag
but I won't put up
with that – it's tantamount
to separate bedrooms.
She tells me it's my height,
the difference between us
that makes this so awkward.
She says she'll take it,
leave me half-in half-out,
one shoulder jostling hers,
the other exposed,

but I'd be left wondering
what people think
of a man who expects the woman
to carry the umbrella.

Raine Geoghegan

THE GREENHOUSE

Mourners spill out into the alleyway. Amidst the black
are flashes of purple and red of women's scarves and
men's ties.

My uncle, a staff sergeant in the army and just back from
Germany is dressed in his uniform. He leans against the
kitchen wall, having a smoke. We drink tea laced with
whiskey. My aunts dry their tears on freshly pressed white
handkerchiefs.

I go into the sitting room and see my sister sitting on a stool,
her hands clasped tightly on her lap. The coffin is open.
Grandfather is in his best suit. His pocket watch hangs from
his top pocket. A family photograph is tucked into his waistcoat
close to his heart. His old hip flask lies at his side, no doubt
there will be a little whiskey in there. He still wears his gold ring.
He looks as if he's resting, as if he'll sit up at any moment.
I place my hand gently on his ...

Grandfather and I are walking down the path to the green-
house. I am six years old. It's a hot day, I'm wearing my
shorts. Weeds and wildflowers tickle my ankles. He pushes
the door open, ushers me in, points upwards. "What d'ya think
of the grapes, my gal?" Tilting my head back I see huge bunches,
deep red, ready to be plucked. He reaches up, pulls a few
down, rinses them in a bowl of water then places them in
my hand. I bite one and the juice runs down my chin.
I eat two more. "They're lovely, Grandfather." He smiles,
opens a can of beer, takes a mouthful and says. "Do ya see
these grapes? Do ya know why they're so tasty?" I shake
my head. "Well it's because the Mulo watches over 'em."
He laughs, I laugh but I'm not sure who the Mulo is.

I finish my cup of tea and tell granny that I am going down
to the greenhouse. The door is slightly ajar, the white paint
faded, flaking. I push the door hard, go in and smell sawdust,
stale beer and decay.

There is an open can of Pale Ale on the shelf, alongside
three broken brown pots. An old knife with a blue handle,
its blade stuck in the wood. It's the one he used to carve
the wagons with. I bend down; pull an old crate out and in
front of me the unfinished wagon. Taking a tissue from my
pocket I wipe the dust off. It's painted red, green and yellow.
Tiny faded net curtains hang limply against the small windows.
The front door has minute horseshoes attached to it. All the
Romany believe them to bring good luck. I would love to
have this wagon. Before I leave I look up to where the grapes
used to grow in abundance. All that is left is a dried, tangled
vine hanging loosely from the roof.

Note: 'Mulo', a Romani word, meaning 'spirit of the ancestors'

Louise C Callaghan

MURMURATION OF STARLINGS

A flock wheels in the reddened sky, ripples and breaks
apart to form once more. At the point of dissolving
it is re-imagined as a falling wave, or a boat
steering the mackerel-clouded sky. Swarm-haze
suspended over a dome in the distance. On the turn
it gleams and flashes, silver steel. Starlings
are guided aerodynamically… in sevens;
between dusk and night stars here in Port Ortigia.
Beyond us then, on the horizon. Nearly out of sight,
a calligrapher's calligraphy. Or held in the mind,
as swathes of charcoal-black on pitted paper,
a lithograph — across a West Cork winter hillside.

Rosie Lavan

REMEMBERED VOICES

Martina Evans, *Now We Can Talk Openly About Men* (Carcanet Press, 2018), £9.99.
Maria McManus, *Available Light* (Arlen House, 2018), €13.

Martina Evans's books are full of speaking voices. Her latest collection, *Now We Can Talk Openly About Men*, emphasises the valency of utterance from the outset and presents two characters whose voices become very familiar to the reading ear. Kitty Donavan and Babe Cronin share this book of seventy-four poems; each woman is assigned her own section, and within the enclosed yet segmented Parts one and two they narrate their personal lives, which are implicated in the larger story of Ireland during and just after the War of Independence and the Civil War.

Kitty is a dressmaker in Mallow in 1919, but drawn back – both in her memory, and in her present perceptions, which are distorted by an over-reliance on laudanum – twelve years to the death by drowning of her husband, whom she now fears she sees again. 'Was that Himself I'd seen on the back / of a Crossley tender on Main Street?', she wonders in the first poem. By the sixth, he has 'appeared again', this time standing beside the 'Royal Red post box' opposite her window. Her troubled conviction enables her to fill in the lost years with conjectures whose toll is physical as well as emotional:

> Small & neat like Himself,
> only yellow, maybe he'd gone abroad
> after his escape, couldn't he have fought on
> the sands of Gallipoli? & the pain
> was kneeing into my brain from the night
> before, as if he had opened my head like
> an egg & was spooning it out. If he
> wasn't Himself then who was he?

Babe Cronin is a stenographer formerly employed in Dublin Castle, which pleases her landlady, Mrs Hayes. She has a passionate attachment to Mrs Hayes's niece, Eileen Murphy, and unlike Kitty she desires another meeting with the absent other, another chance to see the woman she first met in June 1920, in Hayes's Hotel. It is to Mrs Hayes's establishment, and to her disapproval, that Babe returns from London in 1924, the present time of her part of the poem. England has challenged Babe's prim and brittle disposition – 'no / decent work' there 'for respectable /

Irish stenographers'. But, she continues, in an intriguingly elliptic set of reflections:

> I found out, too
> that the English are as bad as ourselves
> & I could not make my way around.
> I shake at the memory of entering
> the soot-black mouth of the Underground.
> But mostly I came back to see Eileen.

That clear last statement is a striking intervention, cutting through those round accumulating rhymes which stitch together a series of unknowns. What is the nature of this equivalent badness among the English and the Irish, we wonder, as poor disorientated Miss Cronin shudders at the thought of those subterranean cavities? Eileen is not without her own unknowns. She is the figure who links the two speaking women of the book yet she does not speak directly herself. Taken in as a child by Kitty, she is then cast out by her because of the Republican commitments in which she will later embroil the devoted Babe.

The circumstances of the protagonists are related yet distinct. Perhaps because of her addiction, Kitty's words evoke a heightened awareness of what she perceives. Her observations are texturised with details which are appropriate for a woman who makes her living by making appearances, and who gets by behind the façade she has constructed for herself and her daughter, Flora. There is a presence about her observations, too, through which we feel the sharp edges of her own prejudices and the narrow limits of a small town made smaller by political divisions. They have the currency and intimacy of a journal; there is always the sense that someone is about to intrude on the inner thoughts of this woman who is fettered by both conscience and consciousness:

> Too much of the elixir that evening
> & the cats still nanging at the sheep's head.
> I couldn't bear to look at them. I had
> a cup of cocoa & Bolands' biscuits
> for my supper before falling asleep
> my head on the large fuchsia pincushion.
> I woke up with dots all across my face,
> I'd have taken more elixir only
> for I'd have had to ask Mr Wrixon
> & that chemist was so fierce narrow-minded.

Babe, too, knows the strain and confinement of negative assumptions. In London, she is 'humiliated. You'd be afraid to open / your mouth. I won't repeat the abuse thrown / at the Irish accent.' In Dublin, under a misapprehension which gradually reveals itself to her – because, she tells us, 'There's not / a single thing in this life that you can't take / in two opposite ways' – she faces the obstructive malevolence of Mrs Hayes, who withholds details about Eileen at the same time as she fails to hide her ridicule of Babe. 'To be treated like an old fool', Babe says, recovering her pride as she remembers. 'To be kept / in ignorance, to be treated like I was mad, / have faces made behind my back in the mirror.' When Babe snaps and Mrs Hayes replies, her words in Babe's recollective monologue – like all the words of other characters in both parts of this poem – are not distinguished by quotation marks, but run freely within the narratives of the speaking protagonists. This somehow intensifies their wounding force, and the overall force of personal testimony these monologues achieve.

Both these women are outsiders; women who talk often are. Babe assents to this status: 'I could never meet the right people', she says. 'I always was & will be an outsider.' Kitty is trapped within her addiction, and assailed by circumstance – it doesn't help that Flora is stepping out with an English soldier. But beyond these details which the narrative affords, these characters represent two of the historically problematised categories of the lone woman: the widow and the spinster. Evans's decision to occupy and represent these women in the midst of a period in Irish history which is at once surrounded by silence and overexposed in the long shadow it has cast, leaves us with a work which is compelling, subtle, compassionate, and evocative. And it has left me wondering about the title: *Now We Can Talk Openly About Men*. We can – and in the privacy of these monologues, which convey Evans's recognised accomplishment in the movement between poetry and prose, these otherwise cosseted women are afforded that freedom too. The title grabs attention – it is breezily current, and admirably witty and weary in its ease. It stands as a knowingly wry heading, issued in another voice, for a pair of dramatic monologues in which two women seek to speak privately about themselves.

Maria McManus remembers voices, too. In *Available Light*, fragments are shored against the advance of time, yet made secure in the ground of allusion. The sound, motion, and luminosity of her poems draw energy from the augurs of the Classical world, who watched the sky and read the future through the movements and calls of the birds. The strokes pulled in these poems which summon the past and are cognisant of the future are deft and often beautiful. For example, the second poem in 'Remnant Nomenclature', the opening sequence of the book, takes its measures from augury and shares between the 'we' of the poem and the 'us' who read it the experience of distance, as irrecoverable memories are pitched in a single sentence that survives line breaks throughout and a dramatic caesura at the end. This short poem starts with a standard secondary school experiment: 'You said, *"Like iron filings and a lodestone"*'. It attains revelation: 'suddenly, we are liminal'. And then it draws out this 'memory measured in luminosity', which is based in the commonplace rebellions of teenage girls:

> adolescents,
> school skirts hitched and rolled at the waistband
> bare-leggéd, absorbed, conducting experiments
>
> in polarities   and magnetism.

That perennially ineffective trick of rolling up the school skirt to maximise the exposure of the leg – an act of defiance which, like so many others, must surely have its origins in the 1960s – here enables an eloquent alliance of the personal and the collective. Like the popular song which never loses its intensity for the individual even though it has given colour and form to the emotions of millions, this is an act which pulls together all the girls who have committed it, even as they are kept apart by generation and circumstance. Carol Ann Duffy's 'The Good Teachers' might stand as an older sister poem, more direct in its anticipation and denied nostalgia: 'You roll the waistband / of your skirt over and over, all leg, all / dumb insolence, smoke-rings'.

Maybe there is some doubleness in McManus's word 'hitched': the comparison with Duffy certainly allows it. 'The Good Teachers' finishes with 'the wall you climb / into dancing, lovebites, marriage, the Cheltenham / and Gloucester, today. The day you'll be sorry one day.' This speculative 'today' is more legible in Duffy's cautionary sketch than McManus's 'tomorrow', given in Latin ('*Cras. Cras.*') and glossed in English in the third poem in 'Remnant Nomenclature'. Tomorrow translates as the inevitable condition of eternal deferment, as McManus manages the Classical references which underpin her vision very carefully:

> and for times when what you need more than anything
> is the perspective only a bird's-eye view delivers –
> with due consideration and without unkindness,
> the answer will be, the answer will always be,
>
> *Cras. Cras.*
>
> *Tomorrow. Tomorrow.*

This condition leaves us full of questions and, as McManus acknowledges in 'The Dark', 'Uncertainty is our inheritance.' What is compelling about her approach in these poems is that her adherence to exploring the experiences this statement encompasses is consistently pliable. The poems are guided by the available light, but they are not arrested at the edge of darkness. This is intriguingly manifest in the sequence 'On Falling', which meditates on Joe Kittinger, the US Air Force captain who jumped from his helium balloon at the edge of space to fall the 31 kilometres back to earth. In the face of this signal example of the excessive recklessness of Cold War ambition, McManus poses extraordinary, simple questions, matching the extraordinary simplicity of the iconic image on the cover of *Life* magazine which captured Kittinger's fall in its daring purity, body against sky. In the fifth poem, '[*A Step*]', she asks, 'Was there a moment / when you thought / you might never wear out / another pair of shoes / or put your cheek / to the earth?' In the next poem, '[*Earthbound*]', the questions take on the grounded urgency of the Chorus of Greek tragedy, eternally powerless witnesses to the most extreme acts of gods and mortals: 'Who kept vigil? / Who waited? / [. . .] Who did not dare / lift their eyes / and look skyward?' In the final poem, enhanced again by McManus's decisive lineation, gravity sets in as she invokes the capacity of the verb at the heart of this sequence:

> And,
> > when a lover's body
> > replied, soft and yielding
> > to your own,
> > did you let yourself
> > > fall then?

Because they are concerned with what cannot last – or, in other words, with the condition of mortality – these poems also present models of what endures. 'The Heart's Graffiti', which gestures towards a form of inscription both ancient and modern, is representative. The poem comes to rest with the encounter between two individuals: 'Listen when a child tells you / she can see her own reflection / in your eyes', begins the final stanza. But it opens with the whole company: 'The living and the dead / are gathering to listen and to judge. / The distance between them seamless', for across McManus's stanza break she finds the collective first person, 'and we go on loving'.

Jenny Carla Moran

I LIVE IN THE VANISHING TRIANGLE

in my room it tastes like cheap cologne and it tastes so strong on my tongue
i don't know   where my skin ends and where memories
begin there are so many photos on the walls
one day when i'm fifteen   i'll say i'll tear
them all down forever because i
hear the women whispering stories about them in the curtains and
when the warm liquids meet down my legs they're
sniggering so before i know which my mouth is i'm
screaming   *i'm fucking alive*
and i know you're a ghost but really

i'm upset that i'm seventeen
already and tasting cheap cologne that tastes so strong on my tongue
i don't know   where my skin ends and where my memories
begin i'm plastered to my wall like a torn photo
leaving gaps in the paint   so blank i
can't tell where right and left are in the dark anymore
but my mother says this is Leopardstown and we have
street lights but no lepers when i'm sad
so i'm glad because i can't tell
where my skin ends and where my insides
begin i squash a handful of blackberries into my
mouth without washing

i'm more hungry since i stopped
taking communion i had to stop because they
said i have to clean all the cum
off my stomach and all the spit
off my face   but i said no
i didn't want to taste the cheap cologne so i stopped
when they said i had to unclench my fist
and let go of the mountains to fit in their doors and
i said no   even though evergreens kept prickling
my palms when a man made me angry but mostly

i stopped when they said i couldn't
ask about all the small dead girls buried under
my hands
if their skins touched the roots

of the blackberry bushes
what they sounded like if they
were whispering in my curtains
what they looked like if their faces
were plastered on my walls
because I knew   the answer to all of those
questions   and i knew
the answer is   no matter
what age i am i still taste the cheap cologne so strong on my tongue
i don't know   where my skin ends and the real world begins

Greg Delanty

MONARCH BUTTERFLY

A monarch has landed on the rainbow deck chair,
presumably taking a breather from her odyssey
of thousands of miles. Dear soul, rest there,

soak up the sun. We know that your journey
has its own cyclops, sirens, Scylla, that you
will need Aeolus' assistance. Silly

to think myth maps apply solely to us human crew.
The blueprint of the House of Atreus
is imprinted deep in our molecules. Many haven't a clue

that the house is coming down around us,
that nature will enforce its own inhuman laws.
The heated gods rally on Mount Olympus.

You fold the V of your wings, hold them in a pause,
hands in prayer, then open and close them in applause.

Janet Sutherland

DILAPIDATIONS I

Snowdrops appeared in drifts, clusters of primroses and daffodils.
We picked them casually, broke their stems. Our cruel hands
stained with sap.

We stole the flowers that grew on paths, the scarlet pimpernels
that blushed the fields. We seized the blooms that closed for rain
or scattered seed when touched.

But every flower of consequence we brought in for our windowsill
drooped in its killing jar. We listened hard and heard the earth
admit the rain. We heard it drink.

Our thieving ears looted the calls of peewits, larks, perpetual
rooks still croaking from their copse, phantom owls, bats whispering
through the dark, the fox's screams.

Pheasants chooked in panic, exploded from undergrowth, but still
we listened without comment, hearing the snarling in the woods
from beaters and from guns.

Lucia Kenny

ROOTS

I walk along hostile streets where
pavements are striped three colours,
and William depicted on his white horse,
grins his no surrender.

My friends are cool towards me,
friendship has to wait
until the drums are silent,
only then is harmony restored.

I'm told not to stray from home,
and not to provoke *the other sort*.
But I am drawn to the loud music
I want to join the marching parades.

If someone sees me
I could be like Peter
and be accused as one of them.
I stay inside and hide my colours.

School days I hurry home before
I clash with the other kind,
lest I listen to their jeers
of spitting names, and taunts.

A Fenian is what they call me,
I shudder as I walk by gardens
of orange lilies.
Only when I'm home do I feel safe.

But days of youth have long since gone
and memories fade with age.
But I wonder does some other child
feel my fear that once was so real?

Or has peace swept in and brushed it away,
leaving only traces of uncertainty?

Milena Williamson

THE OUTING

Did we travel on the north-south yellow
or east-west red? Apart or together
every day we played spot-the-most-tortured
security guard, saint, or gargoyle.
Out of season, we tried a winter dish
of pomegranates, the one that translates
to *beneath a snowy white carpet*. It's
a carpet better shared with you. I wish
we had more souvenirs – an evening gown,
a monogrammed hairbrush, a nameless round
of hide and seek in the balcony room.
The blue canopy bed, an open tomb.
Let's buy walking sticks for when we're women
of a certain age, back home for teatime.

John Greening

HYPERION'S SONG OF DESTINY

    after Hölderlin: Hyperion's 'Schicksalslied'

You tread the light fantastic
   on your sprung boards, holy dancers of the soul.
     Heavenly weather teases
       you, its breezes
         like fingertips of a harpist
           drawing sacred scales.

Unmoved by fate as a sleeping
   newborn, the immortal ones breathe
     safely snug
       in their budding, suitably
        aired, their spirits
         eternally
           in flower and their holy eyes
             looking with peaceful
              clarity for good.

But we have no such luck.
   No chance for the briefest pause,
     unfortunate souls, no –
       we shrink and we tumble
        blindly from one hour
       to the next, water
          flung from precipice to
           precipice, perenni-
              ally down a deeper unknowing.

John Noonan

HYMN OF INNOCENCE

Black prayer book deep
in my pocket
as I cycle narrow roads
to first Mass.
My twelve-year-old heart
unzipping itself, as I peddle
under a stash of bare ash trees slicing the sunrise.
Men in hats throng to the church gate.
I heave the brown door open
into dank-lime wash.
Sitting in silence,
I doubled back to where farm gate
dips to reveal a small lake below.
This is my church on our Holy
Land, a halo of mist –
clearing, the lit font
holding cumulus heavens.

Nicholas Grene

SEA AND LAND

Derek Mahon, *Against The Clock* (The Gallery Press, 2018), €11.95.
Peter Fallon, *Deeds and Their Days* (The Gallery Press, 2017), €11.95.

There had been rumours coming from Kinsale that Derek Mahon had stopped writing. This full and rich book dispels any such fears. In the title poem at the opening of the volume, the poet – now in his seventies – feels himself 'Writing against the clock [. . .] to a final deadline', but takes encouragement from all the artists 'who scribbled on at the unfinished work / with undiminished courage'. Dante, Coleridge, Whitman, Yeats, Akhmatova urge him on:

> 'You thought you'd done, the uneven output
> finished at last, but that wasn't the end,
> was it, since we're obliged to stick it out
> until the pen falls from the trembling hand;
> so just get on with it.'

So get on with it he does.
   This is self-consciously late Mahon. In 'Horizons', he remembers 'When you were twenty-one / you took it for granted you would die young / as genius should'. However,

> Now that you're seventy-five,
> sails idly fluttering, but still alive,
> you sit becalmed, imagining the many
> horizons past and those to come, if any.

In the beautifully complex 'Rising Late', the signature poem of the volume, he wakes mid-morning – 'I don't do dawn / no more' – to the sights and sounds of a New Year's Day that inspires him with his own resolution:

> I would become, in the time left to me,
> the servant of a restored reality –
> chalks and ochres, birdsong, harbour lights,
> the longer days and the short summer nights.

Not altogether a new departure in so far as the last two lines refer to previous collections, *Harbour Lights* (2005) and *Dreams of a Summer Night* (2010). But wonderfully, for a poet who has so often written out of a troubled life, there is a sense in many of these poems of someone at peace with himself.

At peace with himself perhaps, but certainly not with the world as he sees it around him. Throughout his twenty-first century work, Mahon has become increasingly aware of the environment and the devastation being visited on the planet by the destructiveness of modern man. Several major poems here anticipate apocalypse and speculate on a possible future beyond. 'Ophelia' vividly conjures up the hurricane that hit Ireland in October 2017, both during – 'No birds sing in this ominous half-dark' – and after, with the return of electrical power: 'Now lights come on and the fridge shakes, / the phone speaks in a tone of huge relief'. This, though, may be only the first manifestation of climate change to come, with Ophelia in retrospect 'filed as just an autumn breeze, / one of many before the real thing began'. 'Trump Time', however, takes a longer view and hopes for better things. 'Angria', Mahon's term for America borrowed from the juvenile fantasy world of the Brontës, will see its empire come to an end like Tyre and Carthage, Troy, Babylon, and Britain before it. There will be surviving places, 'beloved of poet and artist' to serve 'as temple, shrine and sepulchre'. In these alternative spaces ...

> we live, not in a petulant rage
> for world dominion but an inner continent
> of long twilights shrouded in mist and rain,
> the lasting features of our lost domain.

The current President of the United States is only referred to by name in the title of the poem, but what could better sum him up than 'a petulant rage / for world dominion'?

A part of Mahon's extraordinary power as a poet has always been the catholicity of his imagination, and the eclecticism of his influences. Through *Against the Clock* there are quotations from Robert Graves ('Ninth Wave'), Anthony Burgess ('Homage to Joseph Kell') – Kell was the pseudonym under which Burgess wrote the first of his Enderby novels – Jean Rhys ('Salisbury Avenue'), an imagined monologue by Montaigne, translations of poems by Brecht, and a tribute to the Pogues in the 'Triad for Shane MacGowan', showing once again Mahon's empathetic capacity to go out to the druggies and down-and-outs of the streets of London and New York. Yeats is never far away, often played off in ironic contrast, as with the 'excited reverie' of 'A Prayer for My Daughter' quoted in 'Ophelia', where Mahon contemplates an apocalyptic future with none of Yeats's exhilaration. Late Mahon is very different from late Yeats, happily without the earlier poet's authoritarian rhetoric. The materiality of objects as much as the natural landscape intrigues and attracts the poet.

His poem 'Thing Theory', labelled 'unfinished', makes reference to the school of interpretation pioneered by the academic Bill Brown, defining 'things' as objects that no longer serve their original function. But, with his extraordinary poem 'The Apotheosis of Tins' in *The Snow Party* (1975), Mahon was a thing theorist *avant la lettre*. In 'Stuff' and 'Data' he registers 'the inert, potential force of things material' in a world in which everything can be alive to the imagination.

In his prose collection *Olympia and the Internet* (2017), which serves almost as a companion volume to *Against the Clock*, Mahon quotes the teasing words of Seamus Heaney: 'Why do you always write great poems?' The poems he suggests Heaney had in mind were the early 'An Unborn Child', or the much-anthologised 'A Disused Shed in Co. Wexford'. By no means all the poems in *Against the Clock* are 'great' in this sense; there are occasional poems like 'A Birthday' written for his daughter Katy at forty, or the salute to his good friend and authoritative interpreter, 'To Hugh Haughton Retiring'. But the sense of amplitude and authority in many of Mahon's poems derives in part from his extraordinary mastery of the stanzaic meditation, which can move so flexibly from the informal to the lyrical, from the concrete particular to the broadest level of reflection. 'Mythistorema', its title echoing the work of the Greek poet George Seferis, is one such, in many ways a fitting sequel to 'A Disused Shed'. The contemplation of the abandoned copper mines in Allihies, now commemorated in a museum there, takes the poet to *Lost Mine*, a Cornish painting by Peter Lanyon, and from there to the myth of Orpheus and Eurydice as a figure for the poet's failed attempt to access the past. The poem ends with a plangent requiem for all the dead lives we can no longer imagine: 'Now everyone / whispers together in the dim fields below'. *Against the Clock* is indeed the collection of a great poet, and we have every reason to be grateful for it.

If Mahon since he moved to Kinsale has established himself as the laureate of coast and seascape (in this volume 'Ebb Tide', 'Howe Strand'), Peter Fallon, part-time farmer as well as poet and publisher, has long been associated with the land. Having published his very successful translation of the *Georgics* in 2004, Hesiod's *Works and Days* was a logical place to go next, given that it was Virgil's model for his poem on the farming year. *Works and Days*, though, is an odder poem than the *Georgics*, framed as an apparent address to Perses, a brother of the poet who was given an unfair share of the family property and is berated as a fool repeatedly throughout. It also rehearses mythological stories, such as the creation of Pandora by Zeus as revenge on mankind for Prometheus' theft of fire, and the five ages of man degenerating down from the golden age, before launching into the farming advice and almanac of auspicious dates which make up the substance of the poem. Hesiod was a contemporary of

Homer and, like him, working within the tradition of oral narrative, at a time when writing was just beginning to make it possible to concretise the delivered recital into a permanent record.

Classical hexameters, with their six feet of dactyls and spondees, whether in Latin or Greek, represent a problem for an English-language poetic translator. Reproducing the original can appear laboured and jog-trotty in English, where the shorter pentameter with its iambic rhythm is so much the norm. Fallon himself used a non-dactylic long line in his *Georgics*, while Heaney made brilliant use of a five beat dactylic rhythm in his *Aeneid VI*. According to the 'Afterwords' to *Deeds and Their Days*, Fallon, who does not read Greek and was working from a variety of different translations, made several unsuccessful attempts at his version of Hesiod before coming up with his own distinctive form of six-line stanza, rhyming only on the third and sixth line. 'By discovering and affixing rhymes I shaped a stanza that might allow it to be read as I thought it should be, that is, quickly, with the rhymes as stepping stones in an extended game of hopscotch.' With frequent run-ons from one line, one stanza to another, this does indeed create the onward momentum of a poem originally intended for oral delivery, as in the injunction to Perses on the value of hard work:

> Whatever fortune comes your way
> work enhances it. Don't be a fool,
>   with one eye fixed on other
> men's possessions. Count
> your blessings, pay your way.
>   This is worth listening to, brother.

Occasionally this creates the sort of semi-comic suspense Byron exploited in *Don Juan*: now where will he find a rhyme for that? So we have 'oblivion' / 'live on'; 'gambit' / 'reclaimed it'; 'jar and, yon' / 'garrison'. Internal rhyme, assonance, and alliteration help to root Fallon's poetry in a native English-language tradition: 'the bite and bile / of harm', 'threats and throes of war', and of course the title 'deeds and their days', though pedantically one might object that 'deeds' normally refer to single specific actions, not the seasonally generic work with which Hesiod is concerned.

If we were to seek in Hesiod an idyllically archaic pastoral world, anti-type to the threatened planet of our own latter days, there are disconcerting discordances to be found in the poem. To start with, there is the quarrel of Hesiod and Perses over the division of their inheritance; family disputes over property, it seems, go back as far as the eighth century BCE. Their father was what we would now call an economic migrant from Asia Minor to Greece, 'propelled by appetite / to improve his lot', though

what he found when he arrived was not that much better than what he
left:

> Once he set sail
> from the home place in Aeolian Cyme
> and after a rough crossing set sight
>
> on here and landed. He wasn't
> on the run from wealth untold,
> the easy life, no, not at all,
> but fleeing from the ways of want
> Zeus deals to men sometimes. Near Helicon
> he built a home, a place that some call
>
> Ascra, a backward place, in summer
> bad, in winter worse …

What Fallon slurs over, however, like most modern translators of Hesiod, is the fact that this was a slave-owning society. When you have built your house, Hesiod says (in Fallon's version) 'Then / source an ox to pull your plow / and fix a woman's price – no, / not the one to wed – / to drive your team'. In the literal Loeb translation this is clearer: 'the woman one you purchase not marry'. (There are detailed instructions later on in the poem as to how to pick out a wife). Similarly, what Fallon renders as 'you and your hands' who go out to plough, is explicitly 'you and your slaves'; at threshing time you should 'urge your slaves to winnow Demeter's holy grain' (Loeb), rather than 'exhort the men / to flail the holy grain of Demeter'. Perhaps no modern translator could risk the shock value of the word 'slave' with all its terrible history and its legacies in our time, but it is worth reminding ourselves of the cultural chasm that separates us from the classical world we so often idealise.

Such a level of cultural difference is striking because *Deeds and Their Days* is designed as an ethical, indeed a religious poem. This is its conclusion:

> For he
> is truly blessed and he has all
> the luck who learns the song
> of deeds and their days and holds his head
> up high before the gods, who reads and heeds
> the signs of birds and steers clear of any wrong.

The need to live according to the 'justice' of Zeus, so often urged through the text, involves the due diligence of seasonal work on the land as well as a wary observance of a ritual calendar for fear of divine anger. Hard work no doubt still pays off for farmers at any time and in any place. What we have lost is the reverence and fear for any overriding order of things in the world that might temper the frenetic search for profit. That, at least, is the view of Mahon, whose only deities are the tutelary sun, moon, and stars celebrated in the three companion odes of *Against the Clock*, 'A Bright Patch', 'A Full Moon in May', and 'Stardust'. So instead of the confident belief in living so as to hold the head up 'high before the gods', there can only be the prayer to the sun to 'Shed light on our dark days / with your prodigious rays!'

Marie Morrin

GODMOTHER

I didn't need a reason to go to Number 50.
Sunday, early, I skipped along, the only one, the first,
through the sleepy reservation,
across the wide, deserted bullring,
Divis and Black Mountain at my back.

The newsagent's door clanked open.
A lone, determined dog hurried by.
Another, far off, barked at air.
Each sound ricocheted off sun-bleached concrete,
echoing through stillness into space,
while lazy tyres zipped over melting tarmac.

Through the streets, past the waking houses
I strode, the only one, the first.
A blind went up, a door shuddered.
A collie snoozed in a shady hall,
dreaming on cool linoleum.
Stoves were on. I smelt the gas,
the tea brewing, and the yeasty freshness of toasted batch.

Turning the corner into Whitecliffe,
Number 50's door was open wide, my way prepared
with incense of lavender polish and Brylcreem.
A snore rumbled beneath the stairs.
Bimbo didn't stir. His breakfast, last night's stew,
devoured, the bowl licked to a shine.

Sally rose at once.
She put the teapot on and busied, humming,
between scullery and hearth,
her teardrop earrings twinkling with delight.
The cup of tea, two sugars, was lowered,
handle toward my hand, with a slice of angel cake
for me – the first, the only one.

The sun was at the back at this hour.
A Mass of upturned buttercups in thrall
convened as one with the great white light.

Soon uncle Paddy descended,
and Dee and Trish burst in and we were three.
Linking hands to feet, at Paddy's call
we rolled and crushed the yellow cups,
and squealed, filling their empty sky with atoms of joy.

Terry Doyle

GARDENING IN MUTE
– for Ned

Early afternoon, September
Pre re-education
Uncle Hynes closed in
Showing me through the disused print works
A narrow inclined complexity
Rooms brittle from pressing
Fragile glass in failing timber frames
Up corridors where a headline might go
The compositor's tray now empty
All the words now gone.
Meanwhile in the front garden sun trap
You mutely develop rose bushes
Editing the lawn
Clippings of your propagation leaf forward
You move to the back page
I cut you out and keep you in.

Colin Pink

HOPEFULLY TO DWELL

To dwell is to tarry; stop awhile and just be, be where we are:
perhaps in a dark wood or else alone on an empty strand –
from the one you can't see far, the other stretches farther than hope.

The original meaning of 'dwell' was to make a fool of or lead
astray, like a magician or hypnotist who enchants us to our
cost and leaves us to rue the day we were made to dwell.

In Middle English 'dwell' meant to hinder or delay, like traffic
or the wrong kind of snow that makes a simple journey into
a vexatious string of uncertainties replete with privations.

The present sense of 'dwell' dates from the mid-thirteenth
century, so it's been around, sticking with us, staying put.
Dwell likes itself just as it is, no fancy footwork required.

Ali Lewis

LOVE POEM TO YOUR SELF-SUFFICIENCY

*Stand in a field long enough and the sounds
start up again,*

as they do when
times I sit quiet in another room
and you forget me,
eventually,
and start to hum,

talk to yourself,
cajoling, motivating, praising.

And knowing
that to call attention to a thing
is as often to kill
as to save it,

I say nothing – enjoy
the sound of you, without me,
happy.

Note: the opening lines of this poem are from 'Becoming a Redwood' by Dana Gioia

Gerard Smyth

IDOLATRY

In the gap where the cinema used to be
instead of plush red seats there's a garden of weeds,
a wall of graffiti where the big screen titles
once appeared and the dust of wild stampedes,
heroes and heroines in their close-up scenes.

No stars tonight except the stars above,
no *Snow White* to be a boy's first love,
no whispers in the dark, no music making more suspense
before the duel at sunset or the Gestapo arrive.

Coming out of the darkness
we were light-headed after scenes from the Blitz.
There was always a hero and his nemesis,
tears of mascara when the story got sadder.

In the gap where the cinema used to be –
this was where evenings passed,
afternoons spent in idolatry
watching great wars fought again

or the comedy of errors that raised a laugh,
the Hollywood epic that cost the earth,
the actors who for their parts put on masks
and wore the crowns of kings and queens,
the hats of gunslingers, gangsters, buccaneers.

Phil Kirby

LANDSCAPE / PORTRAIT

That he was born at the foot of a hill
whose name he never used to understand;
its view, the known and unknown world.

That he spent many hours clothed
then camouflaged in shadow-leaves,
in leaves of light, concealed and mute.

That the air he breathed was scented by
the forest floor, the fungal-sweet decay
of litterfall; of leaf-mould and dark earth.

That walking through dry grass released
the summer's sibilance; found him standing
in the ruins of a farm, as he supposed.

That the slopes resolving in an open plain
account for running with abandon, headlong,
till the impetus is spent and all direction lost.

That every rise and brake, each stream,
the very clay beneath his feet became
familiars; a part of what will be his ghost.

That everything comes back to this.

Lottie Limb

BLANAID SALKELD (1880-1959)

Blanaid Salkeld was an orbital figure in early to mid-century Dublin. Across the cultural scene, Salkeld inhabited many roles: playwright, actress, essayist, translator, publisher, and above all extraordinary poet, now unjustly out of print. She wrote four poetry collections in the thirties and fifties – *Hello, Eternity!* (1933), *The Fox's Covert* (1935), *...the engine is left running* (1937), and *Experiment in Error* (1955) – and was a frequent contributor to literary magazines. When I first encountered Salkeld's poetry in Lucy Collins's marvellous anthology *Poetry by Women in Ireland* (2012), I felt gripped by something singular, instantly mobile as only poetic insight can be.

> How are you incommoded, birds, honey-hearted ones!
> Tremulous compliments to each other essaying.
> Barbarously, vibrations of new-fangled engines,
> [...]
> Your lives and your loving thwart, gay, golden throated ones!
> – 'COMPLAINT'

Collins introduces Salkeld as 'the most strikingly modernist' of the poets in her book, and so this thickly textured, archaically syllabic verse makes an intriguing opening. It sets up what Collins sees as a central strand in Salkeld's work: the tension 'between the organic character of nature and an increasingly technological world'.[1] In Salkeld, the celebration of nature is never far from the formal drama of her verse. Though modern stuff is transmuted in interesting ways – especially in the later sequences – one would not turn to Salkeld for documentary: her interest lies with the living beat. Organic forms offer a fruitful entry point to her oeuvre, and self-fashioning. 'Form', printed in *The Dublin Magazine* in 1948, imitates a beehive's enclosed structure in four arch-rhymed quatrains, building upon its quizzical beginning, 'Who stole the bees' hive?'

> Rhyme, the rivet. Hi, Cripple! It is not a crutch,
> Not a spur for the jaded; but the last light blow
> Cheery with accomplishment. As the stars glow,
> Brightly coinciding, each with each, rhyme is such.

---

1 Lucy Collins, ed., *Poetry by Women in Ireland: A Critical Anthology 1870-1970* (Liverpool University Press, 2012), p. 45.

> Were it wise to fling blindly out of metre, past the border –
> (Discipline fetters) – maybe, wrenched free of time's tangle,
> To be rapt suddenly on an eternal angle?
> Who am I to apprehend rhythm? God is order.

This fresh foray into literary criticism's well-worn debate on *vers libre* should not be taken at face value. Beneath the honeyed riposte to neo-modernists lies a genuine creative struggle, as Salkeld plotted her own course between traditional and free verse forms. The antiphonal stance of 'Form' – '(Discipline fetters)' – echoes throughout her career, throughout her war against Time. Rhyme receives more positive treatment: useful and demonstrably beautiful in the imagery of starlight, its connections suggest movements outside of a linear temporality. Salkeld finds further possibilities – and internal 'escape' routes – in its observance. The shapes rhyme makes are integral to her organic form building, most especially in the sonnets of her first collection.

Reviewing *Hello Eternity!* in 1934, Beckett found 'much that is personal and moving [...] when not rendered blue in the face by the sonnet form'.[2] It's an apt putdown from 'the suspiring voice' of Irish literature, but one that misses what is precious and enduring about Salkeld's organic creations. 'Fruit' grows through the tight matrix of a Petrarchan sonnet, producing syntactically pared lines: 'Cool polished rind inviolate, proud fear / Refusing dint or damage – (How impose?)'. Whilst the following 'Autumn' urges 'Love's fledgling' to remember '… how the dark was sweet … / How light and warm the pressure of love's feathers', slowing to capture the primal beauty of this space, in wonder worthy of Gaston Bachelard. 'Unicorn' is, I believe, the most extraordinary of these early poems:

> Not to be shriven – but to be armed and covered.
> I have not dipped my panache in the stream.
> Dawn lifts and lifts and shivers up the clovered
> Meadows and feathered slopes – and lets the lovered
> Sigh in their peace. Nay, hide me from my dream …

In characteristic Salkedian style – reminiscent of Emily Dickinson – the poem opens with an advanced trail of thought, wrestling with its conundrum in a privately symbolic and strangely punctuated way. Its psychic landscape puts me in mind of Christina Rossetti's 'The Convent Threshold' (1862), set in the shadowy hours between desire and devotion. Where such coded language looks off-putting, the intuitive drama of this piece sweeps you in.

---

2 Samuel Beckett, 'Recent Irish Poetry' in *Disjecta: Miscellaneous Writings and a Dramatic Fragment* (Calder, 1983), p. 74.

The careful, discrete poems of her first collection traverse the mythic and the familiar. 'Sea Children' (a sonnet) and 'Home' (thirteen lines), for example, emerge as variations on a theme. They show a movement away from a magical environment – from the 'Wind and sun and cave and crystal pleasure' that concludes the first poem – so that the second appears as a kind of suburban mirror image; no mention of 'sea-children', but a 'Brilliant blue of eye – the salt sea's spraying', lyrically transfused. Again and again, the sea is a source of creative, explicitly female, power. 'I put on sea-shells for you, so you'd know / I had the secret of your origin', declares the speaker in 'One Root'. Over the course of her long career, she is 'not for sitting in [Charon's] swart boat; / But for wide sea-faring' ('Some Lives Exact', from her final collection).

Salkeld's biography underlies this merging of glittering sea worlds and modern life. She has been productively read in transnational terms, since her early life curved between continents. Born in 1880 in Chittagong during the Raj and raised in Ireland, she married an Englishman stationed in Bombay, and returned to Ireland as a widow in 1908. Her love poetry is bold and elusive, often addressing a mute merman lover, dressed in alchemical imagery.

> He will be out of the sea then, flung in salt-licked
> Draperies drying, and circled by ocean herds:
> Dolphins and seals, wave-absolved. I'll call, with the birds ...
>   – THE FOX'S COVERT, II

The Fox's Covert (1935) froths on the page with briny, compounding energy, not letting up for 156 stanzas. Over these, its *abaccaab* rhyming pattern proves flexuous enough for Salkeld's expansive emotions and observations. At times the verse recedes to the everyday, as if generated out of a commuter's daydream:

> On the tram-top this morning every passenger
> Sounded his cough.
> I too coughed change of the weather. The same set stir
> Of similar machines.
>   – THE FOX'S COVERT, XCIX

> In the tram always at one halt she cranes her neck.
> [...]
> Her memories stretch towards that place, like birds that peck
> Where the sheaf lay.
>   – THE FOX'S COVERT, CIX

This last line bears something of Salkeld's love for the Russian poet Anna Akhmatova, whose symbolist lyrics she translated in *The Dublin Magazine*. Like Akhmatova the imagery is crisp, though the influence is casually shown, and the collection wanders stylistically. Sequences encourage lyric self-renewal, and Salkeld's lyrical subjectivity has a specifically zoomorphic quality: it inhabits animal forms and voices. Birdsong in particular elicits a species-crossing empathy – 'warmed, gilded, myself unknow – / Being for an instant that bird' – alighting upon the green thought that 'Love is cosmic consciousness' (*The Fox's Covert*, LXXVII).

Between *The Fox's Covert* and *...the engine is left running* (1937), Salkeld set up Gayfield Press with her son, the artist Cecil ffrench Salkeld. This practice enabled a greater freedom of form that compounds conspicuously modernist tendencies in her third collection: in one work, a bird now calls 'VoyEZ! VoyEZ!' It is a warning, perhaps, of how convoluted these poems can be. The title sequence turns forms inside out, extracting 'spirit fresh' from a sea-urchin's shell and exposing the creative process:

> Now
> henceforth the fear-forsaking
> artist keeps making
> how?
> matter: everything to the furnace (rejection
> mere loss)

Aural patterns convey both the noise of machinery – the 'now' of newspaper immediacy – and the presence of 'God's Hand', guiding the beats. Salkeld positions the artist between these sonic levels, clearing out 'days' and nights' faint metre and false rhyme' ('That Corner'). This melding of fictional levels is typical of her style, in which abstract nouns are buffeted by the elements. In *Experiment in Error* (1955), Salkeld shakes up her metaphysic once more. 'Temporal' is a favoured adjective, as in 'we are left wingless in the temporal wind' ('Escape'), and 'Miranda', where 'the dawn birds sing, / As we lie separate on our temporal shelves'. Although very different poets, Louis MacNeice makes an interesting comparison at these points in his philosophic reach, seen, for instance, in his *Autumn Sequel* (1954). In both, the hard, asyndetic approach to time meets with mixed success.

Though Salkeld's last collection is rightly celebrated for its re-imaginings of myth, sonnets such as 'Arachne' and 'Owl' represent a continuity of interest. Summoning the spider's art, 'Arachne' is self-possessed in tone, 'She could wish centripetal force, though ... to suck / One late fugitive ... into her still centre.' Punctuation is ligamental in 'Owl', too, which takes on a riddling quality by omitting mention of the eponymous bird in the body of the verse:

> I amass silence, silence, as I go –
> Pleasures and piracies ... The tenuous flow
> Of dark dissolves ... I can recover, so,
> The cliff, the cave, the ledge ... then, slow and low
> I settle, shaking time out of my feathers.

As for Irish mythology, 'For Rollo' re-tells the story of King Lir and the transformation of his children into swans:

> At Patrick's call, after nine hundred years, they stepped
> out of the wave –
> the enchantment broken – they told their sins and wept;
> Patrick, too, wept for pity; slipping their bird form,
> four shriveled beings, out of centuries of storm –
> stood up, and fell to death – baptized, absolved from harm:
> May we be safe!

The swiftness of narrative shows Salkeld to be fully in control of her revivalist inheritance, if not inured to its sentimentality. Equally remarkable is the poem's discursive leaps, from ornithological fable to its final image of,

> The bare intricate branches like mathematicians
> tossing about,
> [...]
> tickle the scampering winds – graciously risible,
> working things out.

Salkeld makes an art of exclamation, or the re-hinged question. Here she shows herself adept at easing tone, achieving a lightness of touch in spite of its wordiness. The modulations within this one poem indicate how much is to be enjoyed within Salkeld's collections.

Blanaid Salkeld's zoomorphic lyrics and organic forms provide one route into her poetic development. And yet, recognizing how the clichéd model of 'self-mastery' ill fits a woman whose first collection was published at the age of fifty-three, Salkeld already possessed a rich store of what Bachelard calls 'primary images' – beehives, shells, webs, caves, and nests – and saw their subjectivities. In *A Dubliner* (1943) – a pamphlet featuring a bird's-eye-view linocut of the city by her granddaughter, Beatrice Salkeld – the poet surveys the literary scene. From her perspective, fame-seeking dead Dubliners wish to 'be in the mode, or hoard up riches,' whilst,

> I cry and I fly in my own weather,
> She said; I am not of their feather:
> They never clinked two rhyming straws together.

Salkeld realized the potential of metamorphosis in the modish, male-dominated circles of Irish modernism from the thirties onwards. Visionary, passionate, and now neglected, the time is ripe for her reappraisal.

Rachel Coventry

ALL METAPHORS ARE FLAWED

The moral is generally something to do with darkness
The moral is a response to a failure of character
The moral is it's difficult to say who the wolf is
There cannot be a moral without a story
In this story, the wolf is closing in
In this story, the wolf is a symbol
The moral is you stood too close
In this story there is no wolf
In a wolf there is no story
Anyone who is not wolf
does not get this story.
Up close you are flesh
up so close imperfect
your skin, imperfect
flakes in your hair
no moral,
no story
just you
there.

Michael Dooley

SOLSTICE

At the foot of the orthostat, a pagan girl seizes.
A cotton dress threshing on a line, she whips and flails
In dawn light. Signing the cross, a drunk
Wanders trip-footed to hedgerow.
A child circumnavigates his mother's leg.
The altar she has made by the sun passage,
Of cloth and candle, idol in oak twigs,
Blinks across the enclosure.
She moves in the mangle of a struck cat –
Hiss and flip, scratch-of-earth fingers,
Fluent and mercurial as the triskelion on her leg.
Grange is woken now by the calf-scream of trumpets.
Songbirds halt like Romans
Hearing, for the first time, the Celt.
Figures move for the portal, side-step
Manure of weanlings shushed away at dusk.
And in the throat song, the bodhrán beat of frenzy,
They war with elbow and etiquette for viewing rights
Of a light that may shine through,
And do notice that she has stilled, and is smiling,
Having found her God.

Orla Fay

POET IN A TRAIN STATION BAR

I come across you unexpectedly
as you sit, hidden behind the stairwell,
typing on your laptop.
I have walked onto a film set
where paper doors are punched through
or sliced to reveal their artificiality,
or into a hall of mirrors.
I am not sure which reflection is real.

I do not believe you have noticed me.
I choose to sit very far away
and I wonder what it is you are writing,
so clean-cut and groomed, a winner,
a man who takes himself seriously,
comfortable in your own skin
but with something renegade attached,
a note to your childhood perhaps,

or a slighted card dealt driving
frightful ambition, a Scarlet Pimpernel
or Count of Monte Cristo lost
to this Parisian place now,
sailing past rugged Gallic coast
the bow crashing up and down
on swelling water as you gaze,
knowingly, to horizon.

I digress, look up from newspaper headlines,
catch the back of a figure leaving
through darkened doors. I doubt
anyone has traversed the furthest corners of you,
your hankering for the wild and solitary places,
disappeared, known only to God
in this nameless humanity
where we struggle for connection.

Mary O'Donnell

DOORWAYS

Once there, a week was delicious, slow to pass,
grandparents and aunts open-armed
to us, who arrived each year on holiday.
The trek south from Monaghan long, exciting,
the Blackstairs mountains a final sign
that we were almost there. Once through the door,

across oil-scented ante-rooms, kitchen door
wide, and grandmother remarking how I'd pass
for my mother's younger sister, a sign
of times ahead: resisting, I armed
myself against what mother thought exciting,
fiercely, much later taking holidays

in places that aggrieved her – French holidays,
my love for *la France profonde*, welcoming door
to a bohemian way; but for now, father's parents' exciting
habits – candles, chamber-pots & calisthenics – I passed
through 1930s rooms, the marble mantle armed
with gentle *art deco* vases, aunt's violin, a sign

that music mattered here in Ballyneale, a sign
of quiet reflection. My other aunt, the nun, her holiday
brought abruptly to an end, wept quiet tears, armed
herself again for convent life, through the grim door
to where she pined silently for laughter, a pass
to something glamorous, exciting.

She later dyed her hair, (Morgan's Pomade), exciting
enough to become blonde beneath the veil, her sign
of entering the world. And then our week would pass,
I'd weep in the car at the end of the holiday,
for the fading, soft, Munster voices at the door,
and Margaret and I now filled again, tenderly, armed

to return north, to school and all, armed
again, recalling the house, the hens, exciting
times with doting aunts, who teased us behind the doors.
As in life, the hard and the soft, secret signs
between adults, mother tolerating that week, a holiday
we never wanted to end; and then it passed.

I still think of the armed exemplar of aunts on holiday,
walks on lanes they made exciting, spirited signs
before we went north to pass again through other doors.

Niamh Nic Ghabhann

INTIMATE HISTORIES

Colm Keegan, *Randomer* (Salmon Poetry, 2018), €12.
Elaine Feeney, *Rise* (Salmon Poetry, 2017), €12.
Denise Blake, *Invocation* (Revival Press, 2018), €12.

The cover of Colm Keegan's *Randomer*, designed by Ray Glasheen, features a black pixelated tree in acid tones of yellow and green set against the matt black finish. The edges of this tree soften into strange flickering orange flames. This representation of the natural world as uncanny, bitter, and harsh reflects the thematic focus of the book in several respects. While there are quiet moments of calm beauty throughout – kayaking across Dublin Bay in 'Little Tug', for example, or the 'Fields of trees encased in frozen dew. / The sun a sullen distant heatless disc', from 'January Train' – *Randomer* is a hard collection. Hard in that it is, as the *OED* defines it (adj. and n.), 'not soft, resistant to force or pressure, firm, solid, unyielding, robust', but also (adv.) 'with a great deal of effort, energy, or force; strenuously, vigorously; assiduously; fiercely; (in early use occasionally) intensely, profoundly'. Throughout this collection, published by Salmon Poetry, Keegan presents the reader with a series of images that are often hard to look at, and presumably, hard to recall, using language that is often determinedly ugly. Consider 'Dáil Question', for example: 'In the centre / of the chamber / a gigantic shit. / And nobody is / owning up to it.' Delivered as a performance poem in Keegan's staccato, rhythmic style, this poem becomes present as one of a series of images that appear and disappear in quick succession. Included in a collection, however – words on a page that stay on a page – it acts differently. This is a good thing. The poems give us things that we need to see, and Keegan uses the different registers of poetry (the spoken word, the performance, and the printed document) to ensure that we see them.

Randomer moves quickly between different states of being and emotion. In several poems, Keegan presents an almost overwhelming sense of familial love and connection. This is evident in 'River Son' but particularly in 'Springshine', a tender insight into 'the soft machine of our life', which revels in the energy, wit, and life of his children as they backflip and joke their way around the house. Keegan's attention to the quiet triumphs of everyday life – 'Last night the house was warm without the heating on', and 'The small ceremony / of cutlery thrown across the table' – recalls the speaker in Eiléan Ní Chuilleanáin's 'Swineherd': 'I want to lie awake at night / Listening to cream crawling to the top of the jug / And the water lying soft in the cistern.' Both are poems which have, at their heart, a deep sense of gratitude for survival, and for the peace of the present moment. The closeness of attention to this peace, especially when it is so intensely ordinary, and so easily overlooked, suggests its opposite – a life of chaos and fracture. In *Randomer,* these portraits of domestic stability are set against poems that chart the devastation of homelessness and austerity in Ireland both in the present, and in the recent past.

Many of the strongest poems in *Randomer* delineate these experiences with a keen and unflinching perspective, such as in 'The Weight of Homelessness (or How to Think Like A Homeless Father)', which focuses on the memory of being able to give a doll's house as a Christmas present, the past luxury of material possessions that brought 'neighbours knocking / at your front door to gasp in awe', and 'the pleasure of putting that dollhouse together', dissolved through homelessness. 'Austerity' combines realism – 'This is the day when the landlord calls – / takes everything we have just to answer the phone, / takes everything we have just to pay what's owed, / takes everything we have just to make it home' – with a surreal series of images ('two slaughtered animals, hooves chopped off / heads removed, insides gone, / hanging from the back door of a rigid truck'), to more fully communicate the sense of terror experienced on an everyday level due to poverty and precarity. This experience is also narrated from a more intimate perspective in 'Punk Mother', in which the speaker remembers 'A cool punk mother / in our Ballymun flat, that summer', and the struggle to withstand the pressures of the outside world:

> There was a safety pin in your red tartan dress.
> And I want to forget everything else
> but our closeness as we hid near the press.

Throughout this book, Keegan is concerned with the role of the poet, and what poetry should do. In the opening poem, 'Murder Road', he writes that 'I'm a special arsonist. My job is waking the crows. / I take people's problem and set them free, dark spells on the breeze.' 'This Voice' makes the claim that 'This voice could be absorbed by the establishment, like all / voices are absorbed, but once it knows its place isn't inside / the castle, it'll keep on.' This claiming of territory is, perhaps, to be expected as performance poets continue to make space for themselves within the Irish poetic tradition, but Keegan's claims also seem to place the poet above the world that the poet observes, allowing this position a kind of moral vantage point that risks self-satisfaction. This can also sound off-key when read beside some of Keegan's cutting descriptions of those figures that he seems to place in opposition to the figure of the poet, characters such as 'Uiscebot' whose 'nose / has been shaved off /

by the IMF grindstone / and like a pliant little ploughman dope / he's returned to the yoke', the 'driver, beer-fat' in 'Randomer', or the nameless middle-class aspirant described in 'Decking'. While he is open to celebrating the connections that are 'so ordinary, divine' in 'Heat', and to trace the brutality experienced by refugees at the Calais Jungle in 'Randomer', Keegan is unwilling to extend that sense of empathy to those individuals that are seen as small-minded, greedy, and flattened by the excessive consumption that exists around him.

Elaine Feeney's latest collection, *Rise*, is also published by Salmon Poetry. Like *Randomer*, it contains many poems that feel sharply contemporary and reflective of the present moment, including 'Alternative Truth', which crowds the page with words that perform the double-act of proclaiming truth while actually resulting in equivocation and confusion. The percussive flood of the poem is reinforced by the use of bold type for the repeated word 'truth', which quickly starts to lose its meaning for the reader: '… the whole **truth** and nothing but the **truth** the skirt was short **truth** consent **truth** we'll be serving **truth** any minute now in the parlour the kind **truth** delivering **truth** …'. Throughout *Rise*, Feeney uses different formal structures, fonts, and voices, ranging from the prescient barbs of 'Muse / Amuse' to the clear-eyed lyricism of 'Journey West', making it a collection of exhilarating abundance. There is also a sense throughout that Feeney, like Keegan, is challenging poetic convention and the sense of what a poet can or should do, and in Feeney's case, what a woman's voice can and should do within the Irish poetic canon. The book is arranged in five sections that begin with epigraphs from Seamus Heaney, Sylvia Plath, Nick Laird, Maya Angelou, and Emily Dickinson, reinforcing this sense that *Rise* is a collection which both challenges and embraces a specific literary canon. The book is patterned with images of self-creation that oscillate between pleasure, power, and anxiety. The making-up of the self as both an act of powerful self-control, or of being controlled, is expressed in 'Inventor' ('I gave myself Marilyn eyes / and a light tongue') and 'Whisht' ('Never quite sure of yesterday's mask or how / to retrace kohl lines onto thinning eyelids'), and across the collection in poems such as 'In Montmartre with Degas' and 'and i hope that i don't fall in love with you'.

Most of all, however, *Rise* is a collection which holds the idea of the female body and its autonomy up to the light. In poems like 'Baksheesh' (from the sequence 'Wrongheaded'), there are references to the scandals surrounding the treatment of women and children in Ireland from the foundation of the State to the contemporary moment, but also a searing investigation of the female body as permeable, mutable according to the desires of others, and as something to be put into service. Feeney's charting of these body-histories is countered with images of taking back her body for herself, of images of sexual satisfaction and experimentation, of love, and of pleasure in the self (from 'Gavel-kind' – 'And how bountiful how bountiful how bountiful you are'). These counter-points of the different claims on the female body (the maternal body, the body of a romantic partner, and of a daughter) are heightened and brought to a crescendo point in 'Hindering Hercules' and 'Antaeus', which engage with illness and near-death, and in which the everyday tasks of childcare and household management merge in a near-hallucinatory way with thoughts of what books to read while dying.

Rise is a capacious collection, and it is difficult to communicate a sense of its breadth and scope in a short review. Its title is repeated throughout in poems that point to a historical reference – that of the Easter Rising, and in that, it should be considered as part of the body of work that has been commissioned or produced as part of the Decade of Centenaries, and particularly among the works that have challenged the meaning of this event, both then and now. It is a volume that is as deeply connected and concerned with the past as the present, tipping the reader into different time depths and zones ranging from the timeless ('Before You Begin') to the very precisely dated ('History Lesson'). It is, in many ways, a clarion call of a collection, one which clears the ground for work to come, by the poet herself and by others, but also a book in which Feeney unfurls her skillful, often beautiful, use of language in registers and images of sadness, frustration, anger, love, and hope.

Denise Blake's *Invocation*, published by Revival Press, is a collection of poems concerned, first and foremost, with family and memory. In many ways, the collection acts as an extended narrative of Blake's own family, stretching back to her grandparents and the stories of their lives and deaths, and forward to her sons, their childhood and burgeoning adulthood. The majority of the poems take the form of self-contained stories, memories which are sealed into narrative, reflecting an image from the opening poem 'Layers of Time', in which the narrator observes a small silver heart-shaped rock on the shoreline, and contemplates that 'When I next return / to this place, time will have passed. Slivers / of moments upon moments, fusing into a lifetime.' The collection encompasses Rutland Island, West Cork, Ohio, and the poet's home in Ramelton, Co Donegal, places where Blake has lived, or has visited in order to re-trace some of her own family history. While public or political moments do feature, as in 'The Dream Turns' or 'The Rabble Children', *Invocation* is roughly structured around these places, and they are present in the poems through their imbrication with the poet's family histories.

Throughout the collection, the desire to set down specific memories and to place them very firmly within an orderly emotional arc is very evident. The roughly chronological structure of the book – beginning with stories of grandparents, followed by early life in Ohio with her immigrant parents, the decision to move back to Ireland, the sudden loss of her mother, the poet's own marriage, and the life of her own immediate family – reinforces this sense throughout of a well-worn and established historiography. To an extent, *Invocation* can be read as the poet's attempt to capture these often-told stories, and to preserve them, an attempt that is mirrored in recurring images of careful packing and storage. 'In Times Of Candle Light', for example, opens with the lines: 'It begins with the boxes, unloaded like treasure / from the attic; what has survived the past year, / was the careful packaging enough / to save all from harm?' This sense of protection, however, may also risk undermining some of the work, particularly given Blake's tendency to underscore each narrative with something of a moral coda that directs the reader to the 'correct' way to understand the significance of each individual memory being presented.

However, some of Blake's strongest poems are those in which she moves away from these somewhat overdetermined narratives, and allows the strangeness of a specific moment or experience to be articulated. In 'The Beaching', which commemorates the death of a pod of whales on the shore of Rutland Island, the unnatural dislocation suffered by the whales mirrors that of her grandmother, as much in the broken asymmetry of the lines as in the image itself: 'Those long-finned pilot whales suffered some trauma, / became distressed and confused. And so for her that winter / when told her grownup daughter had died suddenly.' Intimate moments cut loose from bigger narratives are compelling, such as 'The cup, the side plate, the knife, the spoon' in 'Crockery', last touched by her mother and scrubbed and cleared away by the women who arrived for her wake, or her observation of the 'saucering ocean' in 'Lines from West Cork'. The poems that feel most fully realised, however, are those in which she contemplates her own 'mid-life love', as she describes it in 'Love Sestina', and the loss of children who have become adults in 'Beyond the Front Door'. 'Becoming Shepherds' is a funny, tender poem which eschews clichés, and has Blake and her husband trying to herd sheep from their Donegal lawn on their thirtieth anniversary. In a collection that raises up memories of the ordinary – lasagne for dinner, a birthday picnic, coke cans and cold pizza slices – this dewy, wry poem celebrates what Blake describes as 'the strangeness of it all'.

Maria Isakova-Bennett

BREGDAN

Diane's in haematology,
wig a blonde bob, and I weep for next month.

Auntie gave up, week three of chemo –
couldn't lose her lifelong spirals and curls.

Gemma hates hair, shaves her head,
has weekly wax-offs top to toe.

Here's my daughter's first cut, waist-length,
in a bedside trunk.

Just one. I've asked for months,
tug at the fine hairs down his spine,

make him shout out
when I pluck at his beard.

His card arrives the day before my surgery –
love and a single hair.

Note: 'Bregdan', from Old English, *to weave together*

Medbh McGuckian

RESPONSES TO WEATHERING

Magnets, T-shirts, keyrings, calendars,
museums, conferences, summerschools, and now
the sallow beige stamps. So we go
out suddenly into the garden of violence

and all the sky granted, to follow
a cloud from birth to death.
A wall was built to welcome the shade
of a tree as its guest and in this way

recreate a universe. A glimpse
from behind a half-height muted wall
of a found piece of forest posing
as an intact world and a new

spring is written. What names are behind
the many trees for those standing there?
The odd, unmatching trees
are not even straight.

There are waves in the wood
as if they are just about to
really unfold. The thrown-away
spreads itself outward where,

as a last shudder runs through it,
it turns to stone. As the pearl's
nacreous clock is the sand denied
by the pearl: as the aspirin-shaped

sunset is a paradox, like
tomorrow and as different
as the century before us
or the deterioration in the city's

countenance. Your skin tans
to a hard golden brown
as if hibernating. Small
reflections shine on your books

where we taste the sweetness
of time and the coming
of the fullest moment.
Have the windows moved?

The pool had returned to a more
diamond shape. The accumulated
silence is a slowness that radiates,
not a blunt quotation

from academic quarries,
a measure of weather
among the multi-coloured
cars fading like flowers.

Mary Finn

ON SAMOS
      – for Daniel, summer 2013

From my lounger on the white pebble beach
just below the Hotel Cleomenis
I clock you, head up like a seal, making
for the flat rock at the neck of the bay
where you'll haul yourself out, Perseus,
safe past the gorgons, at right, left
and back of you, stretch out your limbs
and steal the best sun on Samos.

But where did the boy Aristarchus go to
for vantage? Where, using only his eyes,
his flat rule and a hank of upland wool,
feet balanced on some glad rock or other,
did he shoot the earth from its element,
send it spinning round the sun?
Which – the wool was adamant –
was seven times our planet's size.

Inconceivable. Ask Copernicus.
It's unwelcome news. The world was never
at home to such triangulation, nor
to having that proud blue ball of ours
relegated, and kicked beyond our ken.
But still it moves; see how it holds
your precious head, you again in
the water, lighting out for land.

Thomas O'Grady

ENVOI

Half-past dawn. Croaked awake, we watch the sky
wake too, lead-grey, with the slow lurching launch
of a half-dozen origami cranes –
great blue herons – unfolding from their swaying

pine-top perch above our ruddy rutted lane.
They breast the air, a fleet of tattered flags
unfurling stroke by rowing stroke against
the wave-cresting wind ... The morning hours pass.

Noontime comes and goes. The tide ebbs and flows.
We eye the glass-bright bay for fabric hung
on creaking frames of ribs and spine – the flight
of tail-trailing kites let loose and blown astray.

•

Our hearts rise with the sinking sun. Dusk falls.
At end of day, we all come home to roost.

Cecilia McGovern

CROSSOVERS

Those guttural consonants
crossovers from Irish,
the thick-tongued s-aitches

made me cringe when they erupted
into school English.
Keeping them at bay –

a lightning detour
between brain and tongue –
called for watchfulness,

a skill great-grandfather
and grandfather
must have excelled at.

The census records show
they were native speakers;
they also show

the rest of the household,
grandfather's children, were not.
A state of affairs hinted at

in my father's enigmatic remark
that we "were the lucky ones
to be learning Irish in school."

Mary Shine Thompson

HOW THE WORLD GOES

Theo Dorgan, *Orpheus* (Dedalus Press, 2018), €12.50.
Matthew Sweeney, *My Life as a Painter* (Bloodaxe Books, 2018), £9.95.
Eva Bourke, *Seeing Yellow* (Dedalus Press, 2018), €12.50.

Eva Bourke, Theo Dorgan, and the recently deceased and much missed Matthew Sweeney share a capacity to see 'feelingly' how the world goes, as Shakespeare's Gloucester put it. Their clear vision owes much to formal, tonal, and narrative accomplishment honed from decades of dedication to their craft.

    Theo Dorgan's literary love affair with Greece is decades long. His book-length, two-part poem, *Orpheus*, is far from his first foray into 'the breath of the real', as he glossed myth, in his 2010 collection, *Greek*. Back then he had mulled over the fate of Orpheus, who had lost his lover to the underworld when he failed to heed the injunction not to glance back at her.

    Now he muses further on the shortcomings of his maestro minstrel. In Part 1 of *Orpheus,* the narrator is transformed into a Corkonian, Dylanesque troubadour, and his Eurydice is also a singer. The couple initially shared the fiction that he was 'the thief // of dreams [...] who'd bring her to treasure'. Age teaches him that they didn't 'share a life'. He had been tone deaf to her needs; their rages and silences wound down to 'terminal / sorrow'. His hard-won insights are two-fold: he did not know himself at all; and the backward glance that cost him Eurydice was not, as he had deluded himself, a measure of devotion, but evidence that he could not give her what she wanted.

    The poem's second part dwells on this realisation. Orpheus, a chastened and now more insightful artificer, sheds modernity and is reinstated in a mythic setting. This shift facilitates reflection on the essential egocentrism of the artist, on love and work, the conflicting cornerstones of humanness (*pace* Freud). With humility uncharacteristic of a son of Apollo, Orpheus concedes that 'it was pride that ruled me / and not my heart'. He has learnt that 'Work is a music all its / own', that art requires him to relinquish agency and be 'instrument, ward / of the god': 'The song sings me & give me pause'.

    Despite the demands of his muse, he settles into a companionable relationship with Rhea, 'the maternal one, methodical. Ingenious too.' The poem has a comedic ending in the Shakespearean sense: a daughter is born to them. Orpheus achieves a precarious compromise between the lyre and the life to be lived; the poem does not dwell on the loss of the visionary gleam, but it is palpable, and the reader senses that the allure of domesticity may be tested.

Orpheus has the psychological complexity of a Jamesian novel, but condensed, and set in the fiendishly demanding Sapphic quatrain form, with 33 four-quatrain poems in each of the two parts. Dorgan has loaded himself with chains, and the poem is all the more intense for that. He has mastered a Hopkinsesque mimetic quality, as 'hawk crashed, brash, black, down from cold heights' suggests. (It is notable that Hopkins's poetic antecedents, like Dorgan's, are Greek. They include Pindar, whose ode form Hopkins borrowed, just as Dorgan stole Sappho's).

The seamless fusion of form (Sapphic), diction (vernacular), and genre (mythic) facilitates multiple readings that refresh the familiar subject. Orpheus's solid structure and narrative provenance do not straitjacket the verse, although they undoubtedly command some predetermined readings: one is that the pursuit of perfection spans place and time; another is that 'time parsed and sieved / will yield gold if you're patient'. Dorgan's superb technical skill succeeds in creating a well-defined world apart, but his poised, vernacular register insists on the intertextual links to the demotic.

While Dorgan's perspective is ultimately life-enhancing, the same cannot be unequivocally claimed for Matthew Sweeney. In *My Life as a Painter*, Sweeney enfolds minimalist stories in verse, stories in which the outlandish and the inexplicable can, and do, happen. He sketches in strong primary sweeps, leaving much untold, and semantic, existential black spots regularly halt readers in their tracks. If his tales have a neat plot resolution – and it is not always apparent that they have – then any light Sweeney casts is at best oblique. Readers will readily identify with the speaker in 'The Message' who, presented with an 'encrypted' message, wonders: 'How on earth was he to / read it?' The answer seems to be, to trust in Sweeney's offbeat psychic reality, because his signal achievement is his ability to see into the life of things with a tragic vision. His literary still-life paintings are *'nature morte'*.

The poem 'Owl Song' recounts a tale of suicide; 'The Bear' pronounces on the pointlessness of existence: 'as if it / would have made any damned difference at all!' 'The Bone Rosary' reports on funerals presided over by ghosts of the long dead. In 'Retribution', Sweeney confronts the lonesomeness of the flesh, the stark apprehension that you live, as you die, alone. However, a humorous jag often disrupts the flow: missing 'the obvious winner in Cheltenham', for example, is what precipitated the speaker's existential crisis in 'Retribution'. In this respect, Sweeney echoes Kafka, whose work he admired, and who saw the comic facilitating an entrée into deeper understanding.

Self-deprecation supplies a doubly serious laugh to 'Mehh!' The title is a made-up term from childhood for an object at once terrorising and replete with 'the spin of magic, / and metaphor', the first sign that the speaker 'was meant to become a makar'. 'Makar' denotes a Scottish court poet or laureate; but I suspect that Sweeney aligned himself with Berryman's Henry in Dream Song 43: 'Listen! the grave ground-rhythm of a gone ... makar? So what!' 'Gone' in this context is slang for crazy, out of it, immersed in work; Sweeney is indeed far out.

Death came to him soon after this book was published, and its imminence is most evident in the book's final poem, 'The Yellow Pole'. Its speaker commands that a yellow pole be stuck 'in the grave / of a poet', and a red lizard and white snake are to 'climb up the yellow pole //... like the flag / of poetry, or of existence.' Poetry, then, is inseparable from existence, since things resembling the same thing – however phantasmagoric – resemble each other.

The road that poetry travels is linguistic. Sweeney, like WS Graham, uses its obstacles well, containing his wild surreality within strict stanzaic form. The effect of formal restraint and the default impassive voice is to confine readers to the eerily still eye of a raging hurricane. Sweeney's desolation row is almost serene.

Eva Bourke has much in common with Sweeney, although their work inhabits widely divergent realities. Both have a strong affiliation to German culture: Bourke was born in Germany and Sweeney studied there. They share an ekphrastic sensibility: their painterly ability enables their readers to see into the life of the scenes they evoke. Both convey a sense of un-at-homeness, of gleaning insight from an outside perspective. But if the one revels in the weird, the other strikes an often empathetic, if regretful, note.

The exceptional strength of Bourke's *Seeing Yellow* resides in its evocation of what Patrick Kavanagh called 'fantastically ordinary incog' speakers. The poem 'Seeing Yellow' is an essay not on the colour's darker connotations (as referenced in Derek Mahon's *The Yellow Book*, for example), but on 'pure, primary pigment ...' perhaps 'borrowed from the angel in Padua'. It is an ode to sunflowers that imaginatively transport an ill, old man from his hospital bed to a yellow field. The collection's final, powerful poem, 'Plans', is dedicated to a deceased beloved. It is crossed with poignant ironies of the roads never to be taken: 'we hadn't finished the last pages yet / [...] yes, definitely we had planned to finish it'.

'Renvyle' is a triumph of technique and tone. It builds suspense over a full twelve stanzas before it jolts the reader to a full stop. The speaker's bus journey snapshots of a Mayo village pulsing with life and particularity is unified, destabilised, and intensified by the rhetorical repetition of 'It wasn't ... it wasn't ... nor was it ...'. Rhymes are subtle (such as the two-syllable rhyme of 'muscles' and 'nuzzled', referring to a mare and foal), and the hyphenation and distribution of a single word over the poem's final two lines enact the tension at the poem's core: '… but it was that I saw my brother / […] saw him turn and walk away and was heart- / sick'. That heartsickness, personalised here, is also the undertow to her keen observations on the 'shadows of cruelty // and shame' of European history ('Heimat').

Bourke marshals an array of technical apparatus. Her occasional long sentences – such as the one accorded an otter in 'Catch of the Day' – are masterfully controlled with judicious line breaks. 'Berlin Diary' conjures a topographical calendar, each month and district condensed into a brimming haiku. Bourke can anthropomorphise a sleeping town with great economy, as in 'Heimat': 'the houses crouched, fearful / as first graders in grey rows'. With devastating linguistic playfulness she depicts both poem and speaker fragmenting in 'Disintegrating Love Poem …' The arrogant, poised voice of the poem's opening lines yields to a final, incoherent *cri de coeur*: 'I an just like ango ne clse / Tugiy thugs cut' (sic). This is not nonsense verse – the quotation perhaps approximates 'I am just like anyone else thinking things out'; rather, it enacts the collapse of language as the linguistic manifestation of the speaker's breakdown.

Bourke, Dorgan, and Sweeney are established poets who have earned respect and acclaim over decades. All three imagine 'authentic' places or states that both disturb and illuminate a dead present by drawing on the submerged, revivifying resources of language.

Mary Wilkinson

STROKE

When brain breaks I die inside a shiny steel cylinder
sealed with Bach.
Outside the day delivers new leaves on trees
dappling sunlight through trusting open windows
while a woman somewhere has strawberry
ice cubes melt on her tongue.
When brain breaks people bring organic hand cream
and purple socks green tea and blood red tulips.
When brain breaks I think of a painting on a postcard
on the wall over my desk at home.
The painting is called Eleven a.m.
I watch jet trails from bed overhead trying to remember
who painted Eleven a.m. while zig-zag graffiti spreads
across a blue slate sky New Mexico nineteen ninety
washed by wind chimes. Sun tea. Sage.
When brain breaks I love the man who comes
to fix it because he knows. My secrets.
The words deleted unspoken thoughts stuck
waiting to be released. He knows how I want
to grab on. Grab on like the way you might trawl lazy
fingers through silky cool water on a barefoot kind of day
where nothing much matters.
Only sky – a faint breeze.

Ruth Esther Gilmore

OYSTERCATCHERS

Where the hills of Carlingford
shelter stone cages,

stained faces and knuckle-worn
immigrant hands,

our souls find back-breaking peace
and unadorned assets,

the tide determines
the turn of the oysters.

With the taste of my work on
my tongue, the miserable cold days,

the miserable hot days
spin out into golden buds;

for me, for the women and men
who work silently with me,

the tide determines
our destinies.

Jo Burns

AS THE SAYING GOES, IT GOES TOO FAST
    – for L

There was a day you held my hand,
the last time ever. I didn't know it yet.
I didn't think and every night you died
then woke next day, further from me.

Now, I peel back flown days,
including your birth one October,
not just unpainting but also scraping nails
down fifteen years, like eulogies.

A childhood too fast to reconsider
of closeness then distance. I know
a house defined by the barks
of two dogs and a far-off mother.

You grew up through my evening stretches
of putting words to bed instead
of you. Your brain grew indecipherable,
a code of hormones, firing inwards.

Here, disturbed in the impossibilities
of latin, maths and physics, you sit
illuminated by the desklamp, where
I travelled often, so far from you.

Justin Quinn

IVANA LOMOVÁ'S NEOREALIST PORTRAIT OF A COUPLE

They are sitting at a café table.
Most of the canvas is a hill covered in snow –
its groves bare, the winter river below,
white-dusted roofs, here and there a gable

(Prague's palaces and mills). And on the top
there sits in miniature an Eiffel Tower.
Lustrous greys, as though after a shower.
This says: most of a marriage is backdrop.

The city's laid out in the large vitrine,
an ornament of their long conversation.
And that each of them is from a different nation
could just be further colour in the scene.

They are white, at ease – equals seated,
agreeing and demurring. From Crete to Dover
social democracy ticking over
in rows of concrete buildings centrally heated.

Their children are somewhere. They are not
bivouacking beside a border fence
in the cold, trying not to give offence.
They are not poised to jump a juggernaut.

And they know this. It forms part of their talk.
They change in answer to the change around.
They respond. They turn themselves into background.
After an hour they go out for a walk

along the river, past the ministries,
the offices and big hotels with porters.
They wander through the city's different quarters
and in their pockets they have several keys.

Christian Wethered

PRESENT

In carpentry I made you a jewellery box.

The drawers have grooves for
Opening and closing on their wheels,
                    The flat bases covered
With velvet.

And when you close them they give
The tiniest thud.

To open the box takes a tug after which
It rolls back open.

I wonder where you'll put your necklace,
Your rings. The bottom drawer is
For pearls.

I hope you like it. Mr Barnhurst

Did most of the sawing.
The sanding was all me –

I used to rub so it went hot.
Mr Barnhurst was almost deaf
So it was hard to get his attention
In a crowd of boys.

He'd clamp it in
And saw the pieces down from a big block.
Sawdust clouded on our lips as we watched.

Thomas McCarthy

FAITH AND STORMS

Medbh McGuckian, *Love, the Magician* (Arlen House, 2018), €13.
John F Deane, *Dear Pilgrims* (Carcanet Press, 2018), £9.99.
James Harpur, *The White Silhouette* (Carcanet Press, 2018), £9.99.

Here are the last three Catholic writers, poets of inestimable value, who are still writing and publishing at a time when Irish Catholicism as a guiding force seems as dead and morally bankrupt as the Communist Party of the GDR. How Catholicism fell from grace, how we fell out of love with it, is an important story in itself, but how it survives here in the moral atmosphere of three brilliant poets is poignant and, ultimately, beautiful. The alert, lively, sensuous poetic intelligence of Medbh McGuckian has been there from the beginning, from that first prize-winning collection, *The Flower Master*, published by Oxford University Press in 1982. It is a different intelligence from that of the two male poets under review here. It is also politically different, with an entirely different sense of political stress and direction.

    McGuckian does not speak to the Ireland we know. Settled as a Catholic in the *Sudetenland* of Stormont, her poems are aimed primarily at the Protestant imagination, at a moral and political centre of gravity that is not visible from the South. Like Akhmatova in her St Petersburg palace, or Antonia Pozzi trapped in the Milanese mansion of her domineering father, McGuckian's work speaks to Louis MacNeice and John Hewitt, to Forrest Reid and Michael Longley. "I can't understand what she's saying," John Hewitt once complained to me, "but I want to understand her." We are only eavesdroppers at the edge of this determinedly Ulster conversation between daughter and father figure. A Catholic Rapunzel trapped on the roof of Stormont and refusing to come down, she has un-braided the hair of her imaginings in an effort to coax the carriers of Quaker and Presbyterian thought to climb towards her, to be blessed in a shower of Catholic allegories. Her imagination means to trap and entangle the very forces that threaten her: her words are not meant to be heard in Dáil Éireann, but in Antrim, North Carolina, Ontario:

> When my reason has recovered
> safer territory, after being overwhelmed
> by miracle, O powerful bard,
> O humble student, my concrete mind
> intends less to control than discover.

Above is how she addresses the great bard in 'Yeats's Fisherman, Christ', yet in 'Converted Church' she explains: 'My under-the-breath prayer / has an angel-maker's church air // of modesty. Whether the name / of the illness is lilac, / radiance is the middle daughter.' None of her works have ever strayed far from the territory of revelation, blessing, refuge, or ecstasy. 'Snowed under by colours', she writes in 'Calico Cat', the chairs add / blue afterthoughts to the twelve o'clock / light and shade.' This is the world of 'puzzledom and wonder'. It is the world of stretched imagination, of perceptions challenged; of descriptions that are entirely intuitive, trusting in imagination and its inviolable laws. In 'The Concept of Common Fame', a wonderful poem, she has laid out the charge sheets against errant women: 'Ann Bird, she has used her pleasure / of me in speeches, she is a creature / that had need to be twice defined'. This is the company of those who test limits, who challenge that sense of propriety and rightness, creatures who are championed only by poets, by writers 'sunk in the sleep of wordliness' ('Statistical Inquiry Into the Efficacy of Prayer'). As confident and dislocated as Pauline Bewick's painting of naked swimmers swimming in the tresses of a water-woman, McGuckian is adamant, consistent, determined, in her method and her thinking. Thus a priest assesses and grades breast-milk for wet nursing, an insomniac goldfish is kept warm from the inside by her books; in 'Breakdown of Letters', the narrator is 'sure // of meeting Martha at the christening', having been chaperoned onto the page by a scrap from James.

Every description is sent to challenge us, every elliptical encounter, every mystique, everything she makes is a sound-producing garment, a poem like a forbidden thing. This is hard going for the John Hewitts, but it was meant to be. The forcefulness and propulsion of Wallace Stevens or Ashbery is in much of this work. Ideas and phrases challenge the reader, tripping-up and tossing the unsuspecting listener. No poem is ever simply an instruction, but every poem is lacquer-work, a string of pearls, dangling from that Stormont rooftop. What a poet Medbh McGuckian continues to be, as brilliant as in youth, the cauldron of her verse still bubbling over, spilling molten gold over us as we climb to get closer, to escape earthly heaviness, to achieve a late communion.

Master-sonneteer, the Teilhard de Chardin of Irish poetry, Achill chronicler and gazer at the heavens, John F Deane has created a real beauty of a collection in *Dear Pilgrims*. Echoes of Herbert and Hopkins, cadences and themes from Middle English, and pilgrimage – above all, pilgrimage – inform and saturate this poetry. His regret at the Irish Church's passing, or, rather, the end of its crowding ('teeming' would be de Chardin's phrase), is poignantly captured in 'Best Western:'

> The convent:
> its neglected aisles, denuded transepts;
> there were prayers here once, touching on how all human flesh
> falls to the all of clay. Now in the walled garden,

> apples and pears have grown small and hard as pebbles;
> the sisters have found rest
> in neat rows, a small white cross their portion …

With a 'trace of a vague / nostalgia', the poet imagines this convent that has been transformed into a 'Best Western' hotel, thinking of the sound of the ghostly convent gardener's wheel-barrow at night. Here is an artist who understands the depth of loss in that passing of Catholic atmospheres. He is a rare witness. There won't be many of them, not in this era of Magdalen Laundries and Tuam Babies, not nearly as many as regretted the passing of Clonmacnoise and Cill Chais in earlier anthologies. Irish Catholicism has lost its literary witnesses, there is no Ponge or Claudel, though Deane's witness may indeed be a rare and important intervention here. This is what makes his work so important, quite apart from the fine verse-craft and high learning.

Deane had a long and secure childhood in the shadow of benign authority, from Achill parenting to near priesthood. It was a functional, not dysfunctional authority: strict but loving teacher-parents, so brilliantly captured in 'The Village Schoolroom' – 'Sin, she admonished them, / comes from our first parents / who cast their guilt on us, and we live in sin and wickedness. / Mother, dead these decades, // I wish for you the radiance of eternity.' His admiration for the steadiness of their parenting is palpable here, and his parents' radiance illuminates all of his journeys and pilgrimages with a kind of Achill sunlight.

The marvellous sonnet sequence 'According to Lydia' imagines a female disciple of Christ, following her Saviour across the parched landscape as she repeats the themes of his teachings: 'as if he bore / quietness in his bones in spite of the earthed resonance / in his voice; the authority, the unaccountable wisdom / that had been concealed somewhere in the Torah scrolls, / the mourners, the merciful, the hungry.' She follows him all the way to the Cross, seeing a glimpse of Him before the Resurrection and its revelation, thinking she's only been tricked by the light. But she consoles herself with the memory of His words: 'hear as a child, he said, that the deaf hear and the blind / have their eyes opened, the lame walk and the dead rise again / and blessed is the one who does not lose faith in me.'

Deane's work here, so enriching, enchanting, so like a pilgrimage, is one of the best pictures ever painted of a secure Irish childhood. Painting this picture, and repeating it, may be one of his great gifts to Irish literature. His faith radiates from that Achill childhood. How blessed he is to have this unending memory of adult goodness. It feeds his faith.

James Harpur is also a poet of faith and pilgrimage. The parenting of his faith, though, comes not from Achill but from an intense adult familiarity with consecrated spaces and ancient manuscripts. I thought that Harpur could never again write a collection of poems as powerful as his earlier *Angels and Harvesters*, but in *The White Silhouette* he has created a book of equal power and verbal authority. Never mind the faith, it is the compelling sweep of narrative here, the dynamic of journeys in page after page, that creates a triumph of contemporary poetry. Like Deane, he has always hovered in the area of the divine, and his lurking in transepts and refectories, in abbey and scriptorium, has created a divine verse-craft. Meditations and observations such as those found in 'Graven Images' and 'Goldsmith' are both moving and disturbing; and a poem such as 'Scribe B' is simply a masterpiece.

> a copy of *Kells*, its Latin words
> processing syrup-slow,
> their tops as trim as hedges,
> redolent of the idea
> that every letter must have beauty:
> the m's aqueduct of arches
> luxurious curves of c's
> the l's delicate eyelashes.
> Each word bore its lineage …

In this poem Harpur is sitting in the Princess Grace Library, Monaco, looking at Folio 183r, Mark 15.24-25, and thinking of the scribe's task, so like his own in the dislocated, peripatetic life of the modern-day poet. In the title poem, a pilgrimage poem dominated by the meaning of that image (the man all in white carrying a lamp in all weathers at Jerusalem's Golden Gate), he journeys from Bishopstone to Patmos, from Holycross, Tipperary, to St James's, Piccadilly, to discover his own white silhouette of faith, his Jesus. These faith journeys seem so urgent, so compelling, in both Deane and Harpur, that they quench our humanist ire, because like him we can 'feel like St John, a sad alchemist / in his lab of bubbling cylinders / who yet again has failed to find / the lapis philosophorum – / I blur my focus / and the less I stare the more I see' ('Verbum').

This turning inward and back is also Medbh McGuckian's intellectual method, or pre-intellectual, intuitive method – 'side-glass you again, / for fear of her not being wholesome' ('Dear Madam Nine') – but for Harpur the truth is in the text given rather than the body taken. He is the poet of Knights Hospitaller materials, a quest for that faraway Grail. Faith for Harpur has always blown in with the Lindisfarne storm. There are many other poems here too of astonishing quality, none without challenges to the reader, but all rewarding our settled consideration, Audenesque poems of school and the impossibility of returning: poems such as 'His Father's Ghost' and 'Portora Royal'.

The White Silhouette is a collection to keep reading until the end of the year at least; it is a book for winters of lost faith and Skellig storms.

Christina Lloyd

AT MACY'S

My ears grow cherry red;
I was too hasty pushing studs
through my lobes.

My eyes water from the sting
of the first posts stapled in.
A toddler, I felt the perforation

only after its sound: gunshot
against eardrum. Mother consoled
me, told me how pretty I looked.

The salesclerk asks if I'm all right.
I nod, return to my reflection,
the faux-diamonds, their shape

so familiar. A register bangs open.
I glimpse my mother in her youth.

Deborah Moffatt

A NIGHT AT THE AVEROF

It is Boston, but it might be Beirut,
or Athens or Baghdad, Istanbul or Ararat.

The old men sit in silence, the young men dance.
Hostilities simmer, generations pass.

Refugees, exiles, opportunists, stateless, displaced,
late into the night, destiny dimming, they wait

in an anonymous archipelago of tables and chairs,
in a dark haze of Arak and tobacco smoke,

the Mediterranean receding, snow-topped mountains
melting, abandoned vineyards withering in the sun.

Always the music is the same, songs from another time,
music that lives forever in the immigrant's mind.

The old men listen intently, heads bowed,
remembering a past they never had.

The young men dance with quiet passion.
Hearts quicken, tempers flare.

A girl in a swirling veil floats across the stage,
bare feet treading softly over broken glass.

Outside, the city is frozen in time, a thin layer of ice
plating the streets, a cold wind blowing in from the east.

Mairéad Donnellan

EXHORTATION

> Oh, let us lose our milk teeth and cut instead
> the strong teeth of hate and love
> — St Catherine of Siena

We have been weaned
on the story of Eve
to keep us on our knees,
anointing the feet of men,
only loosening our hair
to dry between their toes.

Despite meeting Christ at the well,
we tote our pitchers of sin homewards,
stay behind the kitchen door
while the bread we made is broken,
the imprint of our fingers baked out,
they think us grateful for the crumbs
shaken from their cassocks.

Our teeth separate wheat
from chaff, can tell silver from tin,
they gnaw on marble altar rails,
on mysteries, difficult to swallow,
are worn down by the axioms we are fed;
transubstantiation, consecration, damnation,
so now we show our tongues,
hold out for morsels of mercy, grace, love.

Liam Aungier

HEDGEHOGS

They wear their rough side to the world
Untouchables who sleep the sunlit hours
And in the twitching time of night

Resurrect to steal about our lawns
– Clumsy, ridiculous in their thorny armour –
To grub on woodlice, insects, worms.

We notice them, if at all, at twilight
Rummaging in the mulch beneath our shrubberies,
Or as road-kill, rotting on the margins of motorways.

But seldom do we see their sloe-black eyes,
Or know the tender pink of their tongues; these
Who turn introspective each October

And crawl into the thought of themselves
To sleep away a four months' frost, philosophers
Who out-fox the snows of winter.

Nancy Anne Miller

MOSQUITO NET AT ELMA NAPIER'S ESTATE

The mosquito net above the bed,
ghost of a writer who once visited her.

The spirit leaves the body above a caved
in mattress, sunken, about to collapse.

So many fictions dreamt on it. The muslin
ties at the bottom like a mango heavy in

a string market bag she bought in Baptiste.
Hangs like an exclamation mark for

the filmy subconscious more vivid than
the mountain view outside the window.

And more present than the mosquitos
gathering on its airy white slopes at night.

Martin Gale
Over and Above (2017)
Oil on canvas
110 x 60cm

Martin Gale
Beginning of Darkness (2016)
Oil on canvas
100 x 100cm

Martin Gale
On Tour (2004)
Oil on canvas
90 x 90cm

Martin Gale
Weekender (2017)
Oil on canvas
105 x 120cm

Martin Gale
Rescued (2018)
Oil on canvas
130 x 160cm

Martin Gale
Walkers (2016)
Oil on canvas
60 x 100cm

Mary Kathryn Jablonski

HEARTSEASE

In February no one thought that there would be another spring. A jackrabbit crossed the path as we left the funeral. Ice storm after ice storm followed, and the freezing rain encased the road in pewter. Even the cat knew it was the end of optimism, as she stopped chattering at the meagre show of morning birds outside the window. But like sex and war, the greening could not be stopped, and although we planted not a thing, the eyes of our eyes soon realized his favourite flower was cropping up along the steps. And in the second year, love divided these, and the wild pansies multiplied on and on anon. Until a feral rabbit made its nest beneath the lattice, feasting on these tender gems, *Heartsease.*

Kathryn Simmonds

NOVEMBER

When she could do no more than hang
between worlds,
or perhaps it was a slipping
out of time, as if stepping from a diving board
into suspending air,
I put my mouth beside
her ear and urged her free.

And when her little breath gave out
what came was such tranquillity
that I was homesick
for before my birth, and in that moment said aloud
You clever girl,
as if I were her midwife
                              and delivering her.

Jessica Traynor

THINGS BEING VARIOUS

James O'Sullivan, *Courting Katie* (Salmon Poetry, 2017), €12.
Liz Quirke, *The Road, Slowly* (Salmon Poetry, 2018), €12.
Colin Dardis, *The X of Y* (Eyewear Publishing, 2018), €12.49.

The challenge of first collections, as once told to me by a more experienced poet, is not to throw the kitchen sink at them. Often gathered over the course of a decade or so of poetic exploration, debut collections rely on our relishing 'the drunkenness of things being various'. Better that, of course, than a grouping of poems that feel unfortunately familiar. Happily, there is little sense of repetition between these debut collections. James O'Sullivan, Liz Quirke, and Colin Dardis are three poets whose approaches and subject matter could hardly be more different.

 James O'Sullivan's *Courting Katie* (Salmon Poetry), with its cover image of an obsolete computer languishing in an urban dump, seeks to weave poetry from cast-off things; the waste land of youth is picked over for vivid moments and memories, offering surprising vistas. In 'Katie', O'Sullivan captures the heady heights of young love while reminding us of the reality of puke-stained ankles:

> Come away, she coaxed, and I did,
> down Parnell Place, holding her hair
> while she vomited, my left foot lodged
> in discarded pizza, the smell of urine
> in my nostrils, ready to be held myself.

There's humour and wit to be found in the conflation of the mythic siren call with the lucid reality of teenage courtship. A vein of keen observation runs throughout the collection. O'Sullivan breathes life into deserted streets and grey city corners with the love of a latter-day Kavanagh. In 'Those Streets', O'Sullivan's paean to Cork, the atmosphere of that city envelops the reader:

> *Those streets are where I'd neck naggins,*
> where the mist would be worth the warm glow
> of candlelight in some snug, stout waiting
> on a table, *scratched to fuck* ...

These public testimonies are paired with more personal poems, addressed to unnamed others, and dealing with the complexities of modern life and loves. These are sometimes more gnomic in expression than O'Sullivan's more nostalgic or public-facing poems, and while their language is perhaps more fluent and lyrical, there is an occasional sense that the reader is watching proceedings at a slight remove. 'Necropolis', a strikingly atmospheric poem, hints at a landscape of ghost estates populated with the dispossessed. If it never quite allows the reader access to the relationship between the speaker and the subject of the poem, it certainly captures the subject's passion:

> There was more sweat than craft poured here,
> and nights spent sleeping, with muscles sore
> from cutting into Kingspan with a handsaw.

O'Sullivan is at his best when evoking place through deft observations of custom, habit, ritual; in these poems he sets himself apart as a writer willing to seek poetry in the seemingly unpoetic, where 'cans of cider/ still taste like stolen nights spent on bridges' ('The Angels' Share').

From a collection which mythologises the rituals of adolescence and burgeoning adulthood, to one that celebrates the arrival of new life. Liz Quirke's *The Road, Slowly* (Salmon Poetry) invites us to join the poet on her journey through new motherhood. This is a collection which specialises in the intricate and insightful exploration of that life-changing event. Quirke has a fresh and surprising linguistic approach, her lyrical flights deftly balanced by a careful approach to rhythm, metre, and sound in poems such as 'Nova', where a child's instinctive trust is described: 'Little cup of courage, you jump / off the round of the earth, unafraid / to spill yourself but you never lose a drop.'

While these are poems that deal with the deep instinctual love of a new-born, they eschew easy sentimentality and explore parenthood's deeper anxieties. 'Fall at 33 Weeks' takes an unflinching look at physical vulnerability around birth, using imagery designed to raise a shudder:

> She said it was like falling
> on a small dog,
>
> that she felt each rattling jolt
> of baby bones

These poems also deal with the complex emotional landscape of new parenthood, its discomforts, its small resentments, and its terrible (and often justifiable) paranoia, in poems refreshing in their honesty. Notable among them is 'Counterfeit', which records the judgement of a group of women who have come to realise that the speaker's route to motherhood may have been different to theirs. The imagistic flight of the last lines raises the poem above the realm of skilled narrative to something even more universal and affecting:

> I see her hold these facts loose as coins in her palm,
> I see her put those parts of me between her teeth
>
> And clamp down, finding nothing but a lightweight metal,
> a hollow ring, a counterfeit.

This is a longer collection of poems and, as the title suggests, they take their time, exploring the experience of motherhood through a variety of lenses over three sections, with a prologue and an epilogue. Perhaps the divisions of the book are not as accessible to the reader as the poet, but their considered titles speak of the poet's care and attention to the poetic weave of this collection. It's certainly worth taking the time to walk the road with Quirke, seeing life afresh through eyes that 'don't know the horizon'.

In Colin Dardis's *The X of Y* (Eyewear Publishing) we encounter a quirky, singular voice which sets the writer apart from the standing army of Irish poets. Dardis is a student of the minutiae of everyday life, and this collection excels when he takes a microscope to our daily rituals, exploring layers both literal and metaphysical in 'The Peeling of Many Things', where the violence of peeling an apple 'lay[s] bare the savagery / of meat alongside hide', and a Crème Egg performs 'the Dance of the Single Veil'. In 'Missed Flight', grains of sand stuck to a postcard provide a forum to meditate on distance and longing:

> I have produced these dark grains of sand for you,
> taken from Ireland, that you might know a beach.
>
> Atlantic and Irish Sea, we have nothing
> of India, of Timor or Tasman. Forgive us.

Dardis's poems are charged with an emotion which is directed by a restrained sense of phrasing and good rhythmic control. This allows a pleasing sense of ironic detachment throughout, but in certain poems a deep sadness is allowed to spring forth, such as in 'Removal Day', which captures the apocalyptic impact of a loved one's death in its moving final lines:

> When Charybdis swallows, the port drains out;
> the remaining sludge will forever speak

> of history. I'll cling to the fig tree
> and imagine you docked nearby, waiting.
> You cannot pick me up out from the mud.
> I cannot lift you up out of the grave.

There are poems of longing and loneliness here, engaged with the isolation the modern condition can bring about, but Dardis approaches these daily anxieties with a philosophical attitude shot through with wry humour. In 'In Equal Measure', Dardis returns to his examination of the seemingly mundane props of everyday life, contemplating how the contrasting ripening patterns of bananas and avocados can tell us much about human nature:

> Contrarily, an avocado
> cannot come to fruition
> while on the tree.
> It must be plucked
> and in separation
> will it only then
> begin to ripen.
>
> This too, in equal measure,
> holds humanly true.

If there is a criticism to be levelled, it is that the formality of the work's syntax can sometimes serve to undermine its vital freshness. However, Colin Dardis is a unique voice, and the continued contribution of these three poets will ensure that Irish poetry remains 'incorrigibly plural'.

Laurence O'Dwyer

MINKE WHALE

Reading on the rocks below the solar panels,
Max comes running over: A whale!

We scan the west-bound current that seems
a river within the sea, until a wheel of water
rises from the waves, then turns and disappears.

The principal idea is kinship – warping.
The ocean as meniscus; shield.

Think of a battle with arrows falling.
Each one disappears as soon as it touches
water. O world inverted – impossible

to be hurt or maimed. Drills and hammers
strip the lighthouse 'til we pause for tea.

Bread and butter with fermented whey.
Brown Norwegian cheese has a sweetish,
iron tang. Leaning back, the boys are chipper;

the full moon of hunger wanes. It is bright out,
it never gets dark. The solar panels hit 92% today.

I conclude that the Arctic summer
is devoted, almost entirely,
to the beauty of exhaustion.

Elizabeth Scanlon

POST-POST-INTERNET

Post-post-internet, all my eye problems went away,
they weren't dry anymore or running tears either,
post-post-internet I remembered what it was like to wake
and not know what happened in the night.

When did you begin to hear it,
the little radio that never turns off, broadcasting night and day?

Some spill of watercolour
diffuses in the glass –

Watch the dye spool out

      those who have never cleaned think
every old thing must be replaced. Just because
you've never used a sponge doesn't mean
it's not a real thing that works.

Laying cheek to table is soothing.
The grain of the wood.

The baby-having part of life,
the storybooks and butterfat part,
passed in so much money panic, illness, and weariness,
I barely remember it –

      we used to count age in weeks

The skylight I didn't notice until it leaked.

Colette Bryce

           AN AMENDMENT
           Dublin, 2015

```
                    A
                family tree
            with its fine-wire hangers
         in tiers                    is a piece
                            of the history of the universe
                    a trinket mobile
                            suspended from a shelf
                a flimsy wind chime
         of births    marriages    deaths
and offspring,                      ad infinitum.
         An ever-      animate affair
   it shivers      in response
                        to a breath,
                            the slightest    disruption
                    in the air.
```

Colette Bryce

UNTITLED, DUBLIN

Ushered onto the bus by their mother,
two little girls. One with a blonde Labrador
in high-vis vest with the legend AUTISM, the other
forgotten, as the woman bleeps her permit
on the scanner, steering dog and smaller child
who at once erupts in a crimson rage,
rejecting the seat selected by her mother.

The older girl, in glasses like her mother,
sits on a little drop-down seat
facing us all. She is dressed in a cream fur coat
like the pelt of a baby seal, so velvety plush
and so pristine it could be fresh from the shop.
Anxious, finely attuned to the sounds
emitting from her furious sister,

she offers placating words along the aisle,
her face a study in worry, compassion,
disappointment and, yes, loneliness,
the various moods rippling across
in response to a sensitive family radar.
She begins to sing to herself, a traditional song
in a high wavering voice, *Báidín Fheilimí,*

and I notice other passengers
glance up at her, but she sings it quietly, barely
audibly, gazing out at a slideshow of buildings
flashing past in colours on the glass,
sometimes swerving her gaze to locate
the mother and sister, tranquil now
with lowered eyes, counting on fingers.

I want to acknowledge this pensive little girl,
to say "Hey, that's a beautiful coat"
or some such thing to make her smile,
but already I reach my stop and step
through the exit doors and the bus pulls off,
its speed increased beyond my pace, and a thread
is snapped and the moment passes.

Colette Bryce

THE PIGEON

There's a broken pane in the window of my ear,
the act of a vandal: a black triangle.
The pigeons are in and it will take a renovation
to reclaim. Alas, there are no plans pending
and a grey dove peers out early most mornings
through the murk, surveying the street below,
harried commuters slanting to their work.
Where the pigeon retreats to, I don't know,
but often the window holds only unfathomable
dark, and the flag of a black triangle.

It may be, in fact, a succession of pigeons
playing the bird at various points
of its life; like the hair wash scene by Almodóvar
where a woman bows down over a basin
then emerges from the towel a different
actress than before – older, sadder, lined –
like an early photographer rising from the cloak
of her machine to a world devoid of colour.

Annemarie Ní Churreáin

THE DEATH OF QUEEN SCOTIA
    at Tralee, Ireland

                                      Soon the contest begins.
Above Mish Glen I still my horse and gaze down upon gold furrows,
trees skinned silver, a purple river pulsing like a vein.

In the country I am from we unbraid the riches from our dead,
slit open the mouths and linen-wrap the remains,
sprinkling gravesides with incense and milk.

Forgive me Anubis, keeper of weight and scales.
It is against my heart that I must scatter on earth my rival
like the rag-ash petals of a rose.   For loss a loss must be returned.

The rage of Gaythelos is in my bones.
I have been robbed of his living scent, the pure salt pleasures of his body,
the peace of his hand on my belly as I weave new kin from seed.

Imperishable stars are circling.
Already I have seen myself in dreams as the steerswoman of an unnamed boat.
The gods have gathered to face the water.

Beyond these heathers, the bloodsong of the tribe is rising.
At day's end I too will be underground, my head sealed by a stone, heavy as a crown.

In this land who will know to mourn my passing
                      with a painted cheek,
                                a shred of silk,
                                              a lock of almond-oiled hair?

Notes
1. According to legend, Queen Scotia of the Milesians was a pharaoh's daughter who came to Tralee in Kerry to avenge the death of her husband. It is said that she died during the Battle of Sliabh Mish while pregnant as she attempted to jump a bank on horseback. The area is now known as Scotia's Glen, and it features an ancient gravestone inscribed with Egyptian hieroglyphs.
2. Tralee is the location of The Rose of Tralee International Festival, an event held annually to select a young woman to be crowned the Rose.

Helen Meany

CORNERS OF THE EARTH

Tom French, *The Last Straw* (The Gallery Press, 2018), €12.50.
Joseph Woods, *Monsoon Diary* (Dedalus Press, 2018), €12.50.
Leanne O'Sullivan, *A Quarter of an Hour* (Bloodaxe Books, 2018), £9.95.

A little corner of this earth, captured in language at a precise moment in time, becomes a way of reflecting on our place in the world and in life, in three rich collections published earlier this year. Taking the three books together, and reading them in and out of sequence over a number of weeks, has had the cumulative effect of stepping out of linear momentum and self-constructed enclosures to pause, to breathe freely, while being offered, say, a bird's eye glimpse of an Asian city from Joseph Woods, or a mythic hero's perspective from Leanne O'Sullivan.

A photograph of farriers on the Western Front is one of a number of indelible images from poems commemorating the First World War in Tom French's fifth collection, *The Last Straw*. Returning to the trenches time and again, this award-winning poet creates haunting tableaux, making new a subject that has drawn artists for a century, as in the terse lines of 'Father Doyle's Mass for the Dead':

> A biscuit box propped on two bayonets
> in a hole cut out of the side of a trench
> will be his nave and altar and transept.

Places and dates pin down and memorialise forgotten histories: 'The First of July, La Boiselle'; 'Lord Strathcona's Horse at Moreuil Wood, March 1918'. In the same way, his poems set in rural Ireland are anchored by place names, and, in one light-hearted sequence, 'After Hours', by a litany of pub names. From the cutting of bogs to the digging of trenches, Pope's 'spirit of the place', quoted here as an epigraph, infuses the collection as a whole. A number of poems stand out from the numerous domestic and observational ones for their compression and elegant craft, in particular 'Bird' and 'Bank', both, in different ways, preoccupied with men's physical labour, on a building site in England or on a bog: 'There was a rhythm to the cut and catch. / He cut. You looked. He swung. It flew. You caught. / He cut. You looked. He swung. It flew. You caught – / a form of talk that obviated talk' ('Bank').

Equally distilled, 'A Conjugation', celebrating friends' wedding vows, deploys rhythm in a similar way: '*I do. You do. He does. She does. They do*'. Teasing out the etymology and resonances of the verb 'to conjugate', it closes with the couplet: 'as the two leaves of an open book, be / yoked, alike in meaning, a single piece'. While the inclusion of an explanatory epigraph from the Merriam-Webster dictionary may have satisfied the librarian in the poet, it somewhat undermines the eloquence of this imagery.

Childhood memories and elegies for his parents are as central to Joseph Woods's new collection as the international travels that seem at first glance to form the theme of *Monsoon Diary*. From the South Pacific, to China, the Western Cape of South Africa and Chicago, the poems range, almost restlessly, in this fourth collection from the former director of Poetry Ireland, who has in recent years lived in Myanmar and Zimbabwe.

From the opening title poem, with its memories of Yangon, to the closing one, 'Like the Rain in Burma', quietly finishing on a pier in Leitrim, changing locales and settings become the backdrop to an emotional, internal journey, exploring the poet's father's death and the birth of his daughter.

In the first of four sections, poems in loosely conversational three-line stanzas try to freeze-frame his parents in the flow of life: 'Weekday Stowaway' finds him visiting them unexpectedly in their old age, and almost eavesdropping on the cadences and rhythms of their daily rituals. 'After tea, I washed up to a faint bickering / in the living room, which I now know / as the language of love – // *better to be arguing than to be alone*, / as the saying goes, a frustration with what's familiar / a half-century of watching each other in relays.'

In 'A Week of Sundays' he returns to his father's northern hometown, 'which, we both agreed / was dying of its own accord', trying to find traces of him: 'I tried to place you. Instead / all I kept meeting was myself / in shop windows, stravaging // / your streets'. In contrast to the more elaborate, topographical poems in the later sections, such as 'Let us fly away to the famed cities of Asia', with their longer line and verse forms, here the simplicity of diction, almost throwaway on the surface, has an affecting impact.

The 84 couplets of 'Driving to Delvin', replete with memories of childhood, wild youth, and lost friendship, have a propulsive energy as the narrator impulsively drives towards the midlands, on 'the half-remembered trajectory' towards the locale of *The Valley of the Squinting Windows*. 'Taking in the gaps // between buildings that open to hay sheds / and paddocks, a kind of Wild West façade; // a row of buildings then prairie beyond. / And what has happened here in over twenty years? // Unfair of me to freight its one street / with past collisions, and yet I'm trying to lay // something down, a store to set by, / for the long haul back East.'

The intensity of feeling is also apparent in 'With this Waltz', in which his dying father holds on to life just long enough for the poet's daughter to be born. The title and epigraph of the 'close-mouthed waltz' – drawn from the Lorca poem that also inspired Leonard Cohen's 'Take This Waltz' – spark an observation of the cycle of life that is more tender than sorrowful: 'And so in early April she arrived all safe / and perfect and you let go of the reins, / duty done, a last responsibility seen through.'

Death and re-birth are given a mythic, brightly timeless evocation in Leanne O'Sullivan's fourth collection, *A Quarter of an Hour*, in which the brain infection, coma, and slow recovery of the poet's husband, Andrew, become a journey to the Underworld. A loved one's life-threatening illness, lost consciousness, and obliterated memory are experiences that might render many writers silent, yet O'Sullivan has not only found a way into this painful terrain, but has transformed it, in poems that are revelatory and strangely uplifting.

I confess I read this collection in reverse order the first time, as though to be certain that Andrew did indeed pull through; in doing so, the sheer artistry and technical assurance of O'Sullivan's poems were thrown into relief. Also, the subtlety by which she reveals the infinitesimal changes in the patient over time: the day he begins to move, emerging from coma; the first sounds he makes; the first words, building up a lexicon, coaxing memory from sensation.

O'Sullivan's predilection for summoning mythical figures – from the Cailleach, celebrated in her earlier collection *Cailleach: The Hag of Beara* (Bloodaxe Books, 2009), to Orpheus, Odysseus, Perseus, and Oisín – here expands to include elements and emblems of the natural world, animals and wildlife, even the fragile Arctic, all allowing her to step out of time. These shimmering figures remind us of all the lives gone before, other worlds or dimensions, oracles and prayers, layers of past civilisations such as those in the Yeatsian 'Byzantium ...', with its ruin of 'the fabled city'.

Byzantium recurs in the luminous 'Morning Poem' in Section II, charting Andrew's tentative recovery: 'Of course memory began in the garden', it opens, then: 'The things we have seen, the sweet, / accidental parts of our lives stooping largely // in their rough matins. *Where are we now?*' And then gradually, as he starts, from scratch, to match words to things: 'What sound do you make to find that? / What symbol means nothing at all?'

These poems are remarkably distilled, yet expansive; they seem to be reaching for something just beyond their own edges, to a place between the signifier and the signified, where language, sound, and meaning might become unshackled, momentarily or forever – as in the penultimate poem, 'Note' ('Just once let's imagine a word for the memory / that lives beyond the body'), which finishes with the limits of language:

> For I have
> singled you out from the whole world,
> and I would – even as this darkness
> is falling, even when the night comes
> where there are no more words, and the day
> comes when there is no more light.

Anne Tannam

PICKING FIGS

She rings me in the early evening
– my first born lately flown the nest –
to tell me they've been picking figs
from trees growing on his father's land.
She tells me of their plans to *make fig jam.*

I let the phrase settle in my ear,
say it to myself to taste it on my tongue;

close my eyes, see a table set for breakfast
– the winter Spanish sun still warm
across the walls and tiles –
the two of them sitting in easy silence:
one drinking the last of freshly squeezed orange juice,
the other spreading fig jam on crusty bread,

days of such mornings behind them,
days of such mornings ahead.

John Fallon

OUTSIDE CALICO MACK'S

I saw a man killed this afternoon.
He slipped on the scaffolding above the sidewalk
And fell about fifteen floors I guess.
His body burst when he hit the curb.

People gathered at my office window,
Stared down at the mess
And said, "This is so grossing me out."
Some on their cells, took pictures and
Texted: OMG! U GOTTA C!

9-1-1. No, it's 9 for an outside line.
9. Now 9-1-1.
"Emergency. Which service?"
"Third Avenue."
"Between 33rd and 32nd, the east side,
Outside Calico Mack's."
"No, he's dead."
"Three minutes ago."
"You can tell. You just can."
"Mexican. South American. I don't know."
"Maybe 20."

A mother in a mountain village,
An older sister with two of her own,
And his little brother
All reaching up
Picking coffee berries in a valley between Andean peaks.

The ambulance came and collected him in a bag.
The fire department came and hosed down the sidewalk.
A waiter came outside
And erased the bloodied words from the lunch board
With Windex and a pink sponge.
He dried it with a paper towel and rewrote:
Happy Hour 4-6pm
Margaritas–$5.

Simon Ó Faoláin

CÁNÓG DHUBH
    – do Mharcus Mac Conghail

Cros dhubh thanaí thú san aer im' chuimhne,
An chulaith ghruama ort ar nós múnla
Ag ceilt chré umha niamhrach do mhianaigh,
Mianach a raideann do chreatlach ar an stoirm Gheimhridh,
Mianach ag ceiliúradh an fhoréigin dhiamhar san aer id' thimpeall.

Ach ar an dteagmháil is lú dod' chos scamallach
déanann fórsa éigin sa talamh
Daoi cré, éan tuí, fear grinn asat,
An tuirlingt ag cumadh aoire ort
Ó bhéal na talún tur neamhghéilliúl'
Nuair a thréigeann tú neamh aeir is uisce de thimpist'.

Le heaspa tuisceana an déagóra
Ar dhainséar, ar chastacht an tsaoil,
Léimeann tú gan buaireamh ón bhfaill
Don gcéad uair
agus leathann do sciatháin
Don gcéad uair,
gan cheist ná amhras
Ach go mbéarfaidh an t-aer do mheáchan,
Is déanann.

Cuireann méarnáil leictreach An Daingin soir uait
Teaspach is fiosracht ort, go gcasann tú
 – Mar a dhein na hógánaigh thiar riamh –
I dtreo shoilse an bhaile mhóir.

Chonac thú ar maidin
ós comhair an Ché Spáinneach,
Ní le dhá thaobh an bhóthair agat ach a chroílár,
tú suite ar an líne bhán,
meáchan do choirp brúite chun tosaigh ar d'ucht,
do chosa laga ag saothrú gan mhaith,
Iarsma do chlúmh gearrcaigh
ina *afro* áiféiseach ar chúl do chinn,
na cairteacha is na lorraithe
ag tabhairt gach cor tobann timpeall ort,

iontas ort fén bhfústar,
ar nós garsúin ó Inis Icileáin
a chuaigh sna púcaí oíche
is a dhúisigh le fáinne an lae
i lár Bangkok.

Tarrtháladh thú, is cuireadh siar thú
I mbosca bróg
chun an léimt a thabhairt athuair,

Ag filleadh ar do mhianach,
Cré umha niamhrach do mhianaigh,
Mianach a raideann do chreatlach
Mar chros dhubh thanaí ar an stoirm Gheimhridh,
Mianach ag ceiliúradh an fhoréigin dhiamhar
San aer id' thimpeall.

John Smelcer

A LINGERING DOUBT

At the end of the tumultuous sixth day
God fashioned Man – a future victim of Raven's

selfishness and greed. Perhaps God said something or
perhaps He said nothing at all. When He was done

He wiped his brow and sighed deeply. It seems
to me that sigh must still be hanging there.

THE DAY AFTER SATURDAY

On the Seventh Day God rested,
exhausted from the busy work-week.

While God dozed, Raven stropped his beak,
turned an eye-pupil toward Creation.

Polar bears slunk into icy dens
wolves slank with tails between their legs
crabs scuttled deeper into the ice-covered sea
caribou stampeded across the tundra
moose sidled behind spruce trees

and maggots squirmed in their rancid flesh-pots.

John Smelcer

RAVENCOLOUR

In the beginning
Raven was as white as a glacier

But eon after eon
his wings turned black

> his head
> his feet
> his beak
> his claws

In the end

his heart became a coal mine
his eyes two black holes
devouring the universe

        atom   by   a t o m

Author's note: In the mid-to-late 1990s, John Smelcer began a poetry project with Ted Hughes, who was at the time Poet Laureate of the UK. After Ted died, John continued working on poems for the collection and was given assistance from Ted and Sylvia Plath's only son, Nick. After two decades, the collection, entitled *Raven*, is finally coming out in the spring of 2019. It includes a cover blurb by Ted Hughes. Permission was kindly granted by his widow, while Ted's only daughter, Frieda, was helpful in securing the permission. Ted considered *Raven* to be the American cousin to his *Crow* (Faber and Faber, 1972). The book even includes an illustration by Leonard Baskin, whose art graced the cover of *Crow*.

Fióna Bolger

BE CAREFUL WHAT YOU WRITE

              I remember
the shiny red cover
of *Black Beauty* – hardback
gold embossed a precious
grown-up gift

              you told me
now I was so old I
must learn to keep secrets
the full spectrum

              the name
of the brown powder
where the cash was kept
who called and when and why

              did you
know me so little – I
already knew well how
to keep secrets

              my body
folded silently over

Nell Regan

BLÁTH AGUS TAIBHSE / FLOWER AND GHOST: THE POETRY OF MICHEÁL MAC LIAMMÓIR IN TRANSLATION

In December 1949, Micheál Mac Liammóir[1] and his partner Hilton Edwards were staying at the Hotel Royal, Montparnasse, in Paris. There they waited for Orson Welles so they could resume work on his film version of *Othello*. When Welles finally arrived, he and Edwards began 'screaming at each other all day to their own great enjoyment. Their new topic [was] the fact that *Othello* was once more on the financial rocks – how like a recurring nightmare the situation has become',[2] recalled Mac Liammóir. In fact the pair had spent the previous six weeks following Welles's erratic instructions and flying between Rome, Venice, Saint-Paul de Vence, and Marseilles. Mac Liammóir, already an accomplished playwright and prose writer in both English and Irish, began writing poems in Irish from many of these locations, including 'Báisteach ar Pharis Anuas' / 'Rain Falls on Paris'.

from RAIN FALLS ON PARIS
This ease in half-lit afternoon:
Paris spread out under winter
all pearl-grey palace and lean-limbed branch
stippling a low sky,
its air freighted with rain
somehow redolent of mandarin,
… if you catch my drift.

Astringent, heady as wine
that scent, that shade
that nuzzles on milky grey
and leaden cloud,
all freighted with rain.
And gold lanterns, all gold lit,
crowd among skeletal trees.

The rain lets loose in a flash
as it does let loose on Paris afternoons;
with malicious chill
delicious hiss
and a slew of demons in a headlong rush
green-eyed, fork-tongued, fleet feet
all mutter and giggle
from the heavens
streeling down the windows

clattering off the roofs
all lisp on the branches
and skitter on the flags
o! Close the darkening skylight.
o! Put down your head! Forget about the world.

    as BÁISTEACH AR PHARIS ANUAS
Suaric slíochta sásta
an saol seo faoi leathsholas an tráthnóna:
Paris ina luí faoi choim an gheimhridh
páláis phéarla-ghlasa agus géaga seanga iarann-fhuara
á mbreacadh ar spéartha ísle
an t-aer go trom faoi ualach báistí
agus cumhracht mandairíní ann
má thuigeann tú mé.

Go saibhir go géar go blasta nós fíona
an dath is an chumhracht seo
go macnasach go faon ar bhrollach na teimhe liathbháine
na néalta atá
chomh dorcha le luaidh
go trom faoi ualach báistí
agus lóchrainn órga
slua de lóchrainn órga
i measc seang-chrainnte nochta dubha.

Tig an bháisteach anuas go tobann
mar thig an bháisteach i gconaí um thráthnóna i bParis:
go fuar mailíseach
go faobhrach siosarnach
slua deamhan ag marcaíocht le fána
glas-shúileach biortheangach bánchosach
ag cogar is ag gáirí
anuas ón bhflaitheas
ag sileadh leo ar na fuinneoga
ag clagairt ar na díonta
ag briotaireacht ar na craobhacha
ag damhsa aníos ó na leacracha:
ó! dún an fhuinneoigín dhorcha
ó! lig do cheann siar! Déan dearmad ar an saol.[3]

His poetry appeared sporadically in journals such as *Comhar* from this point on, and in 1964 was collected in *Bláth agus Taibhse* (*Flower and Ghost*). Published by Sáirseal agus Dill and illustrated by Mac Liammóir, this beautifully produced book was his only poetry collection. One critic called it the most important of his twenty publications, in either language.[4] The poems, arranged chronologically, are wide-ranging in subject and tone; they are languid, philosophical, and observational; they reference Picasso, Nijinsky, and Lear, among others. They are set all over the world, from Johannesburg to Howth, from Ros Muc to Monte Carlo. The publisher noted the irregular, unusual rhythm of the poems, and that, 'This is the first Irish book, we think, that makes use of the literary form, the prose poem.'[5] Between form and content, the blurb concluded, they were a new departure in Irish-language poetry.

Bláth agus Taibhse has long been out of print, and although Mac Liammóir's poetry was routinely anthologised until the 1970s, it does not appear in any of the influential bilingual anthologies up to and including Louis de Paor's seminal Bloodaxe publication, *Leabhar Na hAthgabhála / Poems of Repossession*. The poem 'Na Cait'/ 'The Cats' was on the Leaving Certificate Irish poetry syllabus relatively recently, but my English-language translations here are the first versions to be published, and an attempt to ask the question about where the work might sit in the canon.

'Báisteach ar Pharis Anuas' is characteristic of many of the poems in the collection. It opens with a description of an 'exotic' location, then a small incident becomes the springboard for a meditation on deeper themes; in this case privilege, betrayal, philosophy, and remembrance (along with echoes of the nativity). From the comfort of his hotel room, the narrator watches as a young mother and her son miss a bus in the heavy rain. He castigates the bus driver and implicates himself, who only minutes before had been relaxing and musing on 'how mellow and easeful, how happy/ this urbane life' is. They will stay in his mind, '*Isolated, the dark rain biting into them / the mother, bitter despair in her eyes / the young fella, a grin on his lips*'. He dedicates the poem to them and asks forgiveness for '*The world and I who forsook them in their hour of distress*'.

When he wrote this poem in 1949, Micheál Mac Liammóir was already a long-established and central figure in Irish cultural life. He had been writing and innovating in Irish for 20 years; his short stories, published in 1929, 'must have startled many readers of Irish at the time with their cosmopolitan settings ... and esoteric subject matter'.[6] As the first director of An Taibhdhearc, Galway's Irish-language theatre, he wrote, translated, directed, produced, designed, and acted in many of the first productions. 'Drama in Irish', Mac Liammóir insisted, 'had yet no public to dictate to playwrights. Thus they were free to shape the drama of the future in the theatre of the imagination – a symbolist drama free from the tyranny of the box-office and the box-set'.[7] His 1928 play, *Diarmuid agus Gráinne*, was considered the best Irish-language drama for the next quarter of a century. Mac Liammóir thought that this was cause for concern rather than celebration.[8] As co-founder and director of the Gate Theatre, also in 1928, his theatre work in English was equally innovative and influential. Mac Liammóir went on to publish several theatre memoirs / travelogues, including *Ceo Meala Lá Seaca* and *Aisteorí faoi Dhá Sholas*, which were 'among the most accomplished of the non-fiction prose encouraged by Irish-language publishers in the 1950s and 60s'.[9] As touring was such an integral part of his life, it is perhaps not surprising that the first aeroplane touches down in Irish-language poetry in 'Amhrán na Maidine' / 'Morning Song', also written during the *Othello* chase around Europe.[10] It contains some of his most striking imagery, as well as a modern-day Jesus.

from MORNING SONG

This morning's light is not casting itself on the earth
so much as rising off the soil, oozing from each living thing
and the cosmos alive:
Rome asleep below me
isn't Rome alive? And if alive isn't it blessed?
Air sweet as milk: earth dark as wine.

Paris to Rome, southbound by plane,
in a comfy airless tube
ersatz leather cushions,
windows like open eyes, sightless
but for milky clouds below and high
above us
the Sun: the golden Mother
mocking us in our pen of steel and glass
browsing the papers while all around nothing
but space ...

as AMHRÁN NA MAIDINE

Ní ag titim ar an talamh atá solas na maidine inniu
ach ag éirí aníos ón ithir ag sileadh as gach rud beo
agus tá an chruinne beo:
      an Róimh ina luí thíos fúm
nach bhfuil an Róimh beo? Agus más beo í nach beannaithe í?
Aer chomh mín le bainne: talamh chomh dorcha le fíon.

As Paris go dtí an Róimh ó dheas in eitleán
istigh i bpíobán compordach gan aer
cuisíní leathar tacair agus fuinneoga
cruinne mar bheadh súile oscailte agus gan aon léargas iontu
ach scamaill bhleachtúla thíos fúinn agus in airde
os ár gcionn

> an Ghrian: an Mháthair órga
> í ag magadh fúinn agus sinn istigh inár gcarcair chruach is ghloine
> sinn agus páipéir nuaíochta á léamh againn agus gan inár dtimpeall
> ach spás ...

As well as the long, irregularly-lined poems in *Bláth agus Taibhse*, there are a number of beautifully achieved shorter lyrics, some of which are love poems addressed to Hilton Edwards. The pair were accepted in Dublin as a couple, and this poem is a rare and early example of a gay love poem in Irish poetry.

> YOUR MOUTH
> I was thirsty
> and found a cup of wine
> to drink of
> but am lonely now after
> that old craving
>
> I was hungry
> and found the bread of life
> to eat of
> but am lonely now after
> that old appetite
>
> I was lonely
> and found your mouth
> to kiss
> I am not lonely now nor will I be –
> except after death

> DO BHÉAL
> Bhí tart orm
> agus fuair mé corn an fhíona
> gur ólas as
> agus tá uaigneas orm anois i ndiaidh
> an tsean-íota úd
>
> Bhí goile agam
> agus fuair mé áran an tsaoil
> gur itheas de
> agus tá uaigneas orm anois i ndiaidh
> an tsean-ocrais úd
>
> Bhí uaigneas orm
> agus fuair mé do bhéal

gur phógas é
agus níl uaigneas orm anois ach i ndiaidh
an bháis.

Bláth agus Taibhse was very well received when it came out in 1964. Mac Liammóir was by now touring the world with *The Importance of Being Oscar* (his one man show about Oscar Wilde), which had finally brought him the international acclaim he longed for. In a review in *Comhar*, Liam Ó Briain, an old friend of Mac Liammóir's and co-founder of An Taibhdhearc, placed his poetry in the context of the three greats of Irish-language poetry: Seán Ó Ríordáin, Máire Mhac an tSaoi, and Máirtín Ó Direáin.[11] Despite the individual attributes of their poetry, none of the three, he claimed, had seen as much of the world, had as much to say, or had bared their soul in the way that Mac Liammóir had in this collection.

Ó Briain opened his review by describing how, when he first met a young Mac Liammóir, he assumed that he was from Ros Muc, because of his accent. In fact, one of the many intriguing facts about Mac Liammóir (not widely known until well after his death), was that he had no Irish connections whatsoever. He was born Alfred Willmore in Kensal Green, London, in 1899, and Mac Liammóir was an ingenious, bilingual riff on Willmore (Son of Big Liam). He had been one of the most famous child actors of his day, and went on to study at the Slade Art School. There he became a devotee of the Celtic revival and attended Conradh na Gaeilge classes. He returned to theatre in 1917 when, partly to avoid conscription, he joined the Irish tour of Anew MacMasters' repertory company. He fabricated an Irish biography, complete with a childhood spent on the banks of the River Lee in Blackrock, Co Cork. Mac Liammóir was also fluent in – and translated plays from – Spanish, German, Italian, and French, but Irish had first hold on him. However unusual his route to Irish may have been, he was not alone as a poet writing in Irish though not born into the language. Louis de Paor, in *Leabhar na hAthgabhála*, points out that one half of the poets in that anthology were not native speakers.[12]

Bláth agus Taibhse was reviewed in more measured terms by the critic and scholar Máirín Ní Mhuirgheasa, in *The Leader*.[13] She commented on the unusual *blas* and the fact that Mac Liammóir was known as a painter, but he now proved that he also had a poet's eye. These two facilities were now working together, and as a case in point she picked out the poem, 'An tAm ar Creathadh' / 'Time Trembles', written in New York, in 1953.

from TIME TREMBLES
In the bare centre of the city the earth can exhale.

This is the ground on which the red man
once stood or lay   here he

was eating drinking fighting love-making dreaming
these are the rocks on which he was
praying dancing fire-making foe-watching
once upon a time
this is the place he fell
no tidings or trace of him here now
but today
between ground and sky it seems there is
a tremble in time itself
trembling
like hawk wing
eagle wing
as they drop from the high blue sky
down through the gilded light of this autumn morning
just as leaves drift off branches
towards us
lit with specks of gold
   [...]
The sun is beating down through the golden air
as it has beaten down for aeons
time trembles like eagle wing
until extinct
it goes to nothing
so that this gilded morning is no more close or loyal to
the high burnished towers of the city
or the avenues' smooth undertow
than to the painted tipi of the red man
or a war cry on the air.

    as AN tAM AR CREATHADH
I lomlár na cathrach tá áit anála fágtha acu don ithir.

Seo í an talamh ar a mbíodh an fear dearg
ina sheasamh nó ina luí fadó agus é
ag ithe ag ól ag troid ag déanamh grá ag brionglóidigh
seo iad na carraigeacha ar a mbíodh sé
ag guí ag damhsa ag fadú tine ag faire ar a namhaid
fadó
seo é an áit ar thit sé faoi dheireadh
agus tásc ná tuairisc air níl le fáil anois:
ach inniu
idir thalamh is spéir shílfeá go raibh
an t-am féin ar creathadh
ar creathadh
ar nós sciathán an tseabhaic

> ar nós sciathán an iolair
> go dtiteann sé anuas tríd an aer ard gorm
> is trí sholas órga na maidine fómhair seo
> mar a bhfuil na duilleoga
> ar foluain leo anuas ó na craobhacha mar bheadh
> blúiríní tanaí órga iontu
>   [...]
> Tá an ghrian ag spalpadh anuas tríd an aer órga
> faoi mar atá sí ag spalpadh anuas leis na milliúin laethanta
> agus an t-am ar creathadh ar nós sciathán an iolair
> go n-éagann sé
> go dtéann ar neamhní
> agus túir arda niamhracha na cathrach
> agus dordán séimh glic na sráideanna i gcéin
> ní fíre ní gaire iad an mhaidin órga seo
> ná pubaill ísle dhaite na bhfear dearg
> ná ceol catha a gcuid stoc ar an aer.

At this remove, *Bláth agus Taibhse* is thrilling to read and to translate, in part because it is so unexpected, but also because of the beauty and revelation of many of the poems. Whether Mac Liammóir was writing about the echoes of Native American culture in 1950s New York, the rain in Paris, or the light in Ros Muc, a rich mix of influences are evident. His training as a visual artist, his work in the theatre, his deep knowledge of Irish and European literature and travel all fed into the work. Christian iconography also features heavily in many of the poems; for example, 'Na Cait' / 'The Cats', an hallucinatory meditation on his own creativity and the draining routine of a touring actor, closes with the nativity scene.[14] 'Báisteach ar Pharis Anuas' was the first poem I translated, as 'Rain Falls on Paris', and I loved the challenge of trying to replicate the sound of the original in English. The imagery in the first quarter of the poem (of the rain and a city in winter) is sharp and the lines lyrical, but after the initial descriptions of a missed bus, the dejection of a mother and child and the narrator's self-castigation, this translator found herself losing patience with almost two further pages of repetition. Although the settings and subject matter in Mac Liammóir's poems are often 'sophisticated' (certainly in the context of Irish-language writing at the time), the resolution of many of these longer poems can veer towards the sentimental, and some references feel outdated to the contemporary reader.

    Hilton Edwards was a ruthless editor of Mac Liammóir's work in English, often – literally – wielding a red pen. "You exaggerate, you'll never learn not to exaggerate. It's in your blood," he told him.[15] However, his Irish was not as good as Mac Liammóir's, and some of the longer poems in the collection might have benefited from his editor's eye. The title poem (15 pages long) was written as Mac Liammóir returned from performing in St Helena. It is a dialogue and a meditation on life, death, and art, but also possibly the least successful part of the collection.

There is a case to be made that Micheál Mac Liammóir's poetry has been overlooked in recent times. Could his experimentation (in prose, poetry, and drama) be one of the precursors to the work of the *Innti* generation, or at least stand as another example of a poet granting himself permission to play around with form and content? It is perhaps wise not to exaggerate the extent of this; Mac Liammóir only published a single collection, and poetry was just one iteration of his extraordinary range of artistic expression. His poems do, however, remain an intriguing, innovative, and idiosyncratic contribution to the Irish poetry canon.

Notes
1 The spelling 'Mac Liammóir' is used throughout the body of this essay.
2 Christopher Fitz-Simon, *The Boys: A Biography of Micheál MacLíammóir and Hilton Edwards* (Nick Hern Books, 1994), p. 160.
3 All originals are reproduced as they appear in *Bláth agus Taibhse* (Sáirseal & Dill, 1964), by kind permission of Cló Iar-Chonnacht.
4 Liam Ó Briain, *Comhar*, Im. 24, Uimhir 10 (Deireadh Fomhair, 1965), pp. 19-21.
5 Cover copy, *Bláth agus Taibhse* (Sáirseal agus Dill, 1964).
6 Phillip O'Leary, 'Contemporary prose and drama in Irish: 1940-2000', in Margaret Kelleher and Philip O'Leary, eds., *The Cambridge History of Irish Literature* (Cambridge University Press, 2006), p. 247.
7 An Bunachar Náisiúnta Beathaisnéisí Gaeilge, www.ainm.ie, Mac Liammóir, Micheál.
8 Quoted in Fitz-Simon, p.187.
9 Kelleher and O'Leary, p. 279.
10 Frank O' Brien, *Filíocht Ghaeilge na Linne Seo* (An Clóchomhar 1968), p. 121.
11 Liam Ó Briain, *Comhar*, pp. 19-21.
12 Louis de Paor, *Leabhar Na hAthgabhála / Poems of Repossession* (Bloodaxe Books, 2016), p. 16.
13 Máirín Ní Mhuirgheasa, *Comhar* Im. 24, Uimhir 6 (Meitheamh, 1965), p. 7 (reprinted from *The Leader*).
14 Translation forthcoming in *The Stinging Fly*.
15 *Selected Plays of Micheál Mac Liammóir* (Catholic University of America Press, 1998), p. xi.

Thanks are due to Cló Iar-Chonnacht for rights permission; to Aifric Mac Aodha for advice and encouragement; to the Trinity Centre for Literary and Cultural Translation, where an early draft of this essay was presented; and to Cathal Ó Searcaigh, for bringing the collection to my attention.

Richard Tillinghast

I TUNED UP SEÁN'S GUITAR
  – *for Thomas Lynch*

I tuned up Seán's guitar
        and gave it an airing
                on the flagged forecourt outside Lynch's house,
the wind whipping off the North Atlantic
                three fields from where
   Clare drops into the sea.

Soon I had it ringing
        with songs of my own country,
green mountains, bottomless rivers, deep valleys
        dark as a dungeon and damp as the dew.

I shot a man in Reno, I sang,
        just to watch him die.
                I had no fiddle to liven it.

The foal's whiteness was something not of this world.
Not till tomorrow would she feel
     on her coat, that was new as anything,
   what we call rain.
Camilla licked the foal's sylvan
        leaf-like ears
as I sang out those dire things
   that happened *ten years ago on a cold dark night.*

Even the black crow left off cawing
        when he heard about the long black veil and the
night wind that moans
        and the living who weep over gravestones.

What business had I
        singing into those still-damp ears
ballads of murder and horseback journeys,
    duels and scaffolds
        from a country she had never heard of?

It was some comfort to know
she and I shared no common tongue.

FEATURED POET: ROISIN KELLY

Roisin Kelly was born in Belfast, brought up in Leitrim, and now lives in Cork. Southword Editions published her first volume, the chapbook *Rapture*, in 2016. In the same year her work was shortlisted for the Hennessy New Irish Writing Award, and she was featured poet in *The Stinging Fly*. In 2017 she was awarded the Fish Poetry Prize, and was a runner-up for the Patrick Kavanagh Award.

In the standard questionnaire given to poets in *Poetry Ireland Introductions: 2016* her answers are – as her poems can be – wayward and thoughtful. The question: *Someone offers you €1,000,000 to never write again: what is your response?* Her answer is concise: *Without writing, there's no point. If that sounds bleak that's because it is. I would much rather never write again and writhe around laughing in a big pile of money forever. Unfortunately, that is not the version of the world I live in.*

The version of her world is made clearer in these two poems. Both, but especially the first, *In America*, show a remarkably energized Janus-faced project. The first face looks to the structure of a lyric that has learned from the past. The cadence, the line length, the breaks and pauses all gesture to lyric time. The poem begins with the speaker driving in the US, moving away from the erotic and persuasive world left in the rearview mirror and powerfully, lyrically described:

> Orion stalks the black tops of pines with his starry bow
> but I'm so far from the land where I left you. Last night,
>
> as we smoked a final joint by the lake, Orion, the Plough,
> Gemini, seemed to shed themselves star by star into the water
>
> [...]
>
>   I persuaded you
>
> to lie down & put aside your bow, slipping each
> of your belt's three diamonds into the dark lake of my mouth.

But if the language and structure seem to adhere to lyric convention, the speaker is far away from it. This is a transgressive speaker, whose models have more in common with a disruptive Plath-like narration than with a lyric voice.

The same is true of the second poem here, *Domínio Vale do Mondego*, an artful pastoral of a Mediterranean landscape, with the speaker still distant, estranged and resistant to consolation. The double effect of these poems gives them both poise and power.

The terraces in this valley are ancient.
Pine needles make quiet the old Roman road.

When I close my eyes all I see is olives, falling.
And you, bending to pick up a lamb

just as the pink terraces of dusk begin to fade

Roisin Kelly's work has been widely published. In August of 2018, the *Los Angeles Times* reviewed *Rapture* in admiring terms, acknowledging its unsettling energy: '*Rapture* is hard to read, because we've been where this painful collection insists on taking us. Kelly, as great writers do, compels her readers to engage.'

– Eavan Boland

Roisin Kelly

IN AMERICA

I spend my first night driving through upstate New York.
Miles & miles of highway & car beams blinding me.

Shadows flit by the highway, as if I'm pursued by the creatures
from that strange dream I had on the plane.

Orion stalks the black tops of pines with his starry bow
but I'm so far from the land where I left you. Last night,

as we smoked a final joint by the lake, Orion, the Plough,
Gemini, seemed to shed themselves star by star into the water

& in gathering their points of light you became the hunter
who held an entire universe at bay. I persuaded you

to lie down & put aside your bow, slipping each
of your belt's three diamonds into the dark lake of my mouth.

This morning, waking on wet grass,
we found the tracks of new constellations around our bodies

where deer had passed in the night, unnoticed.

Roisin Kelly

DOMÍNIO VALE DO MONDEGO

You beat the branches with a stick, so that olives fall
as quickly as the days are passing.

Every night at the press: the smell of crushed olives
like warm darkness you could eat.

Here they eat their bread with olive oil and salt.
At dawn the olive nets are glittering with frost.

The harvest must be brought in before the solstice,
your flock of sheep must be brought in before the night.

The terraces in this valley are ancient.
Pine needles make quiet the old Roman road.

When I close my eyes all I see is olives, falling.
And you, bending to pick up a lamb

just as the pink terraces of dusk begin to fade.
A shepherd, a farmer, efficient and practical man.

But more than anyone, you know how an hour
has no meaning: there is only a sheep and its bell

ringing in the distance between you, and the time left
in which you can find it. In this village

of shawled widows, who might they call *witch*?
At the river I write your name on an apple,

cast it in water as black as your name.
Turbines pause in turning on the mountain,

their red bulbs glowing on each blade.
Above the Spanish border, an eagle is floating – forever.

Olives rise from nets and hover mid-air.
Now: is it day? Is it night? It is neither.

The air is a pure colour.

Maureen Boyle

THREE WAYS OF LOOKING AT A POETRY COLLECTION

Kate Dempsey, *The Space Between* (Doire Press, 2016), €12.
Elaine Cosgrove, *Transmissions* (Dedalus Press, 2017), €12.
Alice Kinsella, *Flower Press* (The Onslaught Press, 2018), £9.

At a time when the themed collection is becoming ever more popular, and when the end result can sometimes seem rather sterile, an intellectual exercise only, all three of these debuts suggest other ways in which collections can be organised to include poems which appear written out of more felt imperatives.

 Kate Dempsey's debut collection, *The Space Between*, published by Doire Press, is a warm, expansive book from one third of the Poetry Divas, a women's poetry collective which performs around Ireland and seeks to blur the line between poetry of the page and of performance. What is clear from these poems is that nothing of the page poem is sacrificed in that process. The book encompasses a life – as befits a relatively late debut – starting with love and ending in love, with all the richness of experience in between. Dempsey waited fifteen years to publish in book form, but this only makes the collection's structure all the more satisfying, since there is a sense of chronological progression from poem to poem, but also a clear sense of the range of her voice. Poems of childhood include the fable-like 'While it Lasted', which parodies female self-effacement; and 'The Belt', which captures brilliantly a terror thankfully unknown to schoolchildren now, itemising the various infractions that a child could commit that would invite the 'sleeping black mamba' to be unfurled and unleashed:

> if you were late
> if you chewed your hair
> if you spoiled your jotter
> if you forgot your homework
> if you mixed up your letters
> if you sang out of tune

There are tender love poems here to her husband, from the romantic early days to the later days when changing the loo roll or hoovering become part of clever, witty observations about married life. There are poems that mark the coming of children, while the beautiful poem, 'The Flight of Swallows', includes the wish of a mother that she could take suffering from a child. In 'Snow Women' there is the sense of the sometimes 'bewintered' relationship with an older child. Wit is definitely a feature here – and satire. There are two very funny poems about male poets (or possibly even the same male poet), who 'needs someone to mind him, / listen to and forgive him – / God forbid – sleep with him' ('Drunk the Poet'). Dempsey started as a scientist, and there is a short sequence on the elements, plus a beautiful paean to Oxford, where she studied: 'I knew a city with golden stones, / a place of scholars'. I think some of the best poems evoke Dublin in all its sensual ordinariness – the smell of the sour hops in 'Essence', a build-up of traffic on the M50 in 'By Strawberry Beds'. As befits someone who values the public performance of her work, she is good on rhyme, both end and assonance, so that the poems read naturally and easily. This is a rich, rewarding first collection.

Elaine Cosgrove's *Transmissions*, published by Dedalus Press, though the debut of a younger woman, still carries something of the same sense of chronology, beginning with poems of becoming and of movement. The opening poem, 'Motorway', is luminous in its description of what the poet sees from a bus, the light through trees 'a society of brightness', the 'immeasurable world' passing and mutable, and the self wanting to be effaced. The second poem of the collection, 'Endless', speaks of how 'We become in spite / of what happens, and / we are here, still here / becoming with care, / and listening [...] endless in this sudden / glittering world of interruptions'.

Cosgrave's poems fizz with detail, with the concrete, ideas are conveyed through things, through stuff. Her teenage years are remembered in 'Eighteen', when the 'kingdom of youth' is a place among 'darkened bluebells in the forest behind the house', and youth is entranced in a spell of 'garland lights, our dwelling, joints and gin'.

Her native Sligo is invoked in poems like 'Surfing at Streedagh Strand', which links her own experience of the beach with a dark story of the plunder of one of the Armada ships, and the abuse of the sailors washed up there. The savagery of this poem is brilliantly linked as a dark threat in the imagined future of the contemporary lost-at-sea, at the end of the following poem, 'The Crossing'. The West of Ireland is there also in 'Cruinniú', a fabulous poem about a different kind of transmission in language, this time Irish, and which recalls Gillian Clarke's 'Miracle on St David's Day', in a more mischievous – but then tender – tale. This poem is typical of her work in terms of its always surprising imagery:

> Their kestrel-brown school pinafores attempt to lift at their hems
> with sharp swerve of the rolling Atlantic breeze.

'Anatomical' is a gloriously rich and detailed prose poem full of colour and depth, broadcasting from 'the secretive city of the heart'. The poems are full of movement, dislocation, travel, and the vulnerability that comes with that, as for example 'The Loop', which ends with the girl who is the 'I' of the poem taking a well-trodden route to 'Leeds, Liverpool, London' over 'the green sea that banishes me', asking, in the poem's affecting ending, 'do you know I will be safe? / Do you know to the taxi-man, to the nurse, / to the magazine in this eggshell blue waiting room.' 'Reservoir' is a poem in three columns remembering 'my people' who lived in the megalithic tombs under the Hudson, creating the reservoirs of New York, while 'Systole, Diastole' uses the opening and closing of the heart's ventricles to evoke the anxiety of a sleepless night. This is a stunning debut of young life and energy moving towards a possible resting place, 'my peering point', at the end.

And finally, Alice Kinsella's *Flower Press*, from Oxford publisher The Onslaught Press, is a collection of poems that form a single narrative of loss, grief, and survival. This book is physically beautiful, a complete artwork, taking the idea of the 'Flower Press' – a brave title, given its possible sentimental associations with Edwardian ladies – and using it to create poems that are indeed fragile distillations of memory, words held 'between pages', preserved. The book is beautifully structured, starting with an epigraph, 'Bias', in which she registers her shock at seeing the public commemoration on social media of someone she loved, 'A URL, a date, a wall of comments', and ending with the title poem with its reflexive reference to how,

> Someday, I'll open up this book
> and be glad to find
> these long-lost printed
> skeletons of you.

And so the intervening poems, dividing into sections of 'Bud', 'Bloom', and 'Blood', and lusciously illustrated by editor Mathew Staunton, reclaim her own version of the lost friend, starting in childhood with one 'found...in the garden, / the first day after we had moved in', the boy she 'looped the lane on new bikes' with on Christmas Day and who brought back shells from holidays 'to share a little of the sunlight with me'. Poems like 'Messiah Frog' in the childhood section take on a darker, foreshadowing tone when you have read the whole. Or, 'Oisín, little deer bard boy' in 'Tír na nÓg', of whom 'no amount of love / could keep him in the land without death'.

In the extraordinary 'No lamb can take away the sins of this world', the birth of winter lambs is witnessed: 'Soft slap of flesh on cold concrete, / the limp wet blue thing, ruined red ewe / bowing to kiss away amniotic gunk.' The poem ends with: 'You told me we weren't supposed to get too attached, / but I did, that was always my problem.'

The sequence 'Bloom' moves into teenage years in Mayo, where Kinsella grew up; the poem 'Confession' remembers hiding-places among the silage bales of the West:

> I told him that the smell reminded me of cows' breath
> and late winter morning trips to see early-born calves
> with a boy I was supposed to have forgotten.

'The Art of Forgetting' is a prose poem which perfectly enunciates the ways we try to handle the past and how we move between tides of longing to return, wanting to pick up the phone or turn up at the door, but in the end, don't. And this sequence ends with the stark,

> But when your loss came,
> I could run only home,
> the pull of it too strong,
> to face what love had done.

The final sequence, 'Blood', describes precisely and movingly the confusions of the early days in the aftermath of tragedy – 'a clash, a clatter, a scream' – followed by the wake under a 'pierced painted heart', where 'Only your face is still, / pale in eternal solitude. / It is quiet.'

The elegiac nature of this section reminds me of Hughes's *Birthday Letters*, especially Kinsella's speculating on how much might have been different, how much was seeded in their early lives:

> It was planted for us,
> eight years on,
> six feet down.

The bravest poem of all, perhaps, is 'Separated', which does that difficult thing after a death of claiming her life from death:

> I'm not like you,
> we are different kinds now.

Its final line reads as a manifesto for her own poetic life too, with all its evident promise:

> I am pure potential.

Lex Runciman

NEWS, 1949

And so she poured the clear libation
        over the rattle and cracking welcome
                of cubes of ice,
and with soda watered that liquid,
        and for herself opened an amber bottle
                and in the same fashion poured,
in that one expectation of the happiest of effects,
        and soon those glasses filmed with thinnest fog
                as the air warmed.
The life we have made is good, she thinks to herself,
        the kitchen fire well caught, alive
                in darkened windows, white and red
and yellow. Their table set, candles in place, the plates,
        knives, the four-tined forks, and by now,
                by steady sips that first glass has emptied –
she pours a second, even then turning
        as she hears a car motor arrive and switch off,
                a door opening, a door closing, footsteps,
and she is poised, calm, ready.

Billy Fenton

HEALER 2

Red patches all over my face.
Ringworm for sure, they declared.
Took me to a faith healer,
better than any doctor, they said.

Deep in the countryside,
in a dark cottage, maybe a cave,
he turned a wheel to stoke a fire,
reached for a burning stick,
glowing end, curl of smoke,
pushed it towards my face.
I started to cry, pulled away.
They held me, cajoled me,
he approached again,
whispering magic words.

They brought me one more time,
my face turned back to white.

A cure passed from father to son,
since who knows when, they said.
I wonder now, fifty years on,
if it's lost, was he the last,
the one who took it, to the grave?

Heidi Beck

AN ENDING WITH FOOD AND FLOWERS

Imagine a last dinner, Valentine's Day.
Imagine the two of you.
Observe how he cooks you jasmine rice
and Thai green curry, creamy with coconut.
Observe the bouquet of pink carnations
speckled with a mist of baby's-breath.
You are so lucky, people say,
He cooks and brings you flowers.
You are so lucky, your husband says,
I cook and bring you flowers.
I am so lucky, like the happy ending
of a film.

        Consider though how many times
a particular meal is prepared in a marriage.
Consider that this curry is always too hot.
Feel how the fire starts on the tongue, smoulders
through the nasal passages, hollows the ears.
Feel how the breath hitches, the eyes run,
and how the heart accelerates away.

Cut to the flashback, where you ask him please
not to make it so hot again and again and again.
Cut to the flowers, fresh and pink and blameless
but for reasons particular to you, they resemble
scar tissue and are scented with the lack of love.
Understand that he knows this.
Understand.

Kathleen McCann

CROSSING TO ENGLAND FOR HARVEST WORK

> There were those who were brought over as ballast, 'huddled like pigs,' others were landed secretly on the Welsh coast before the vessels reached port and dropped by night, in the mud ...
> – Cecil Woodham-Smith

Fever, exhaustion, hunger's
hitch, conjures an urge to
sink, give in
to the mud's seductive
suck and pull; drop
to the knees,
lower the head
and let go.
Let the mind blow out;
bright breath, body's
bee, float away.
Effortless, nonchalant
wave of the hand,
a grand day.

Emer Lyons

CORK CITY, 1974

My mother goes to a disco in a bridesmaid's dress,
attracts unfinished men,
men with only one eye, one arm, one leg,
men I see in photographs dragged down from the attic,
when the past starts to cave in the ceiling.

She doesn't know what to do with them,
they sit in the corner of the kitchen for weeks,
memories that have no place in the present.

I want to be a photographer,
I take pictures of flowers up close, far away,
of the dog, the cat. I buy black and white film,
photograph colourful things, explain to people
when the pictures develop, that in real life the buildings are green.

Some are so hazy, I can't make out the subject.
I try to hold my hands concrete still, but there's always a slight shake.
I start to research Parkinson's, Alzheimer's.

Certain moments she rescues from the kitchen corner,
frames and places, on bookcases obscuring the hardbound Dickens
nobody reads, on tray tables atop doilies already littered
with dusting carafes, wedding crystal. The glass inside one frame
smashes but it gets left there, shattered on display.

I look at the pen etched into their backs, denoting date and place,
in case one day in the future there'll be cause to remember
that in 1974, you, mother, were at a disco in Cork City.

Paul Bregazzi

TALISMAN

A big country-hand made from drumlins and barbed wire,
squeezes into the bone – digging the badger of sorrow

from the deep. As if personally responsible:
"Sorry for your trouble." He covers himself again.

Another holds your hand and bicep like a shield worn against the throng.
Delivers the long message: "She knows all the secrets now."

Out of the corner of his mouth to the uncle:
"Looks like they've started pullin' from our pen."

A distant cousin: "You'll know the meaning
of a lump in the throat now."

Grave words; a hex against the hollowness
when a handful of earth hits it.

Lorraine Carey

STARCHED SHIRTS

My father owned countless white shirts,
pristine, bright as new snow and starched
when my mother was in a good mood.

Robin's starch clung to the kitchen air,
partnered the hiss-cloud of steam
from the heavy iron; the coiled flex

like his wife, tightly wound and frayed,
dismayed the electrician in him.
Sometimes I took over and tried,

sprayed the collars, the sickly smell
of Monday nights and solitude,
when she escaped to the bingo hall.

Placed them on wooden hangers,
the collars perfectly stiff with approval.
He seemed to collect shirts, as I did comics.

Displayed on the left-hand side
of a wardrobe overflowing
with handbags, glad rags, even packets of Shag

bundled, elasticated, concealed,
surprised him when his cigarettes ran out,
not enough of a lure though, to keep him home.

I counted the shirts and his hours away,
listened to the fire and for a taxi's hum,
the engine's rattle, the nod to flee.

Abandoned the task, hurried to fold
the ironing board and disappear,
as he tried to walk in a straight line
and navigate the house plan in the dark.

Bernard O'Donoghue

ONCE IN A LIFETIME

Seamus Heaney, *100 Poems* (Faber and Faber, 2018), £10.99.

One way of measuring the prominence of a poet is the stage at which selections from their work begin to be made, and the frequency with which they appear. Selections from Yeats – and even some volumes of his *Collected Poems* – appeared from early in the twentieth century, over thirty years before the completion of his corpus. By the standards of modern poets, Seamus Heaney's first *Selected Poems* came early, in 1980, drawing on poems published in the ten years from his first major volume, *Death of a Naturalist* in 1965. *New Selected Poems 1966-1987* appeared in 1990, and the handsome, substantial *Opened Ground: Poems 1966-1996* came out in 1998. Most recently, a second volume of *New Selected Poems* to supplement the 1990 volume was published in 2014, the year after the poet's death.

Importantly, the editors of that second volume of the *New Selected Poems*, as well as including the selections from *Seeing Things* and *The Spirit Level* the poet had made for *Opened Ground*, were able to draw on the selections Heaney had made from the volumes after *Opened Ground* for a prospective volume of his poems in Italian translation. This is important because it involves the poet himself in the selection. It is particularly important too in Heaney's case because, on the evidence of his papers in the National Library of Ireland, he was inclined to summarise and plan selections from his poems from early in his career, from the publication of *North* in 1975. (He famously said: 'up to *North*, that was one book'). Now, in the 'Family Note' at the start of *100 Poems*, a selection made by Heaney's immediate family, his daughter Catherine tells us that he 'had contemplated such a book, particularly in later years, and had gone as far as discussing it with his editor and close confidants. The notion of a "trim" selection appealed to him'.

So what he have here is as near as we can get to an authorised, personal selection of that kind. The first thing to say is what an extraordinarily impressive and attractive collection this is. *The Guardian* comment on the cover says that Heaney was 'the greatest poet of our age', and it is hard to think of a poet of our age from whom as powerful and varied a collection could be drawn. Catherine Heaney says, in the 'Family Note', that the 'selection is imbued with personal recollections of our shared lives' within the family; and, insofar as it is possible to generalise about the spirit of the selection, the personal poems are strongly represented. For example, the moving elegiac haiku '1. 1. 87' is included here, though not in *Opened Ground* or the *New Selected Poems*:

> Dangerous pavements.
> But I face the ice this year
> With my father's stick.

Heaney is a great and generous elegist; there could have been more of the sequence 'Clearances' in memory of his mother; but an inevitable inclusion from them was the sonnet voted in 2015 as the nation's favourite poem, 'When all the others were away at Mass'. It is not just a family preference that leads to the inclusion of so many personal poems; Heaney had a great gift for personal poems celebrating family and friends alike. Another inevitable inclusion here is the great poem 'Keeping Going', in tribute to his brother Hugh. The other great poem for Hugh, the sonnet 'Quitting Time' from *District and Circle*, is not included, perhaps because it covers the same ground. A hundred poems would be a spacious allowance for most poets, but there is strong competition for inclusion in Heaney's oeuvre.

Besides, there is strong competition between the kinds of poem the oeuvre contains. Heaney was a great personal poet; but he was also a major public poet, to an unusual degree in English in our time. The Troubles poems have to be represented – like 'Casualty', and 'The Strand at Lough Beg' – which combine the public and the personal-familial. As early as 'The Other Side' in *Wintering Out* (1972), he was giving eloquent expression to the possibility and difficulty of good neighbourliness in rural society in Northern Ireland. The family editors have not flinched from the political power of poems like 'Funeral Rites', with its terrible oxymoron 'neighbourly murder'. He is a poet too of the historical moment: the poem of 9/11, 'Anything Can Happen', or the lines from *The Cure at Troy* quoted by Mary Robinson and Bill Clinton:

> But then, once in a lifetime
> The longed-for tidal wave
> Of justice can rise up,
> And hope and history rhyme.

The favourite poems are well represented here: 'Digging', 'Follower', 'Mid-Term Break', 'Broagh', 'Postscript', 'The Monks of Clonmacnoise'. A useful function of the appearance of this trim selection now is that it is a platform for later poems that have had less time to work their way into the nation's bloodstream: 'A Call', 'At the Wellhead', 'The Blackbird of Glanmore', 'Miracle', 'The door was open and the house was dark' in memory of David Hammond. These poems may come to compete in popularity with 'Digging' and others: in the course of a reading of 'Digging' in Sligo shortly before Heaney died, when he paused hundreds of audience voices carried on with an impromptu choral murmuring of the poem while the poet looked on in genuine astonishment. Heaney is the rare case of a contemporary poet with a claim on real popularity. A striking case of a poem included here because it has developed its own popularity beyond the earlier *Selecteds* is 'Scaffolding', which has over the years become a favourite at weddings. It was one of the very first Heaney poems to receive a wide publication, in the *New Statesman* even before *Death of a Naturalist*. Its inclusion now is acknowledgment by a kind of plebiscite.

Even if there is nothing here whose selection is contestable, every Heaney reader will have poems and lines they would like to add. Like Yeats, he has an unsurpassed capacity for the general truth: 'How perilous is it to choose / not to love the life we're shown?' ('Badgers'); 'Like the disregarded ones we turned against / Because we'd failed them by our disregard' ('Mint'); the family heirloom 'willable forward // Again and again and again' ('The Settle Bed'). This mythopoeic capacity which exalts familiar things into wide general truths is illustrated here of course: the poet's father's advice to his sister travelling to London, 'Look for a man with an ashplant on the boat', is both grounded and mythological – cattleman and deity.

One of the considerations for the family editors was to select poems that were 'among his favourites to read and which conjure up that much-missed voice'; in that way the book is a timely associate for Geraldine Higgins' moving and evocative exhibition, which opened this year in Dublin and which similarly conjures the voice. Byron said: 'A great poet belongs to no country; his works are public property', and this book reminds us too how a poet can be private as well as public property: national as well as universal. It is a rich, perfectly-judged sample which, beyond its familial focus, radiates outwards in the multiple directions that the work takes us.

Mícheál McCann

HOOK-UP

Rural Donegal

Lonely people waking
to scroll through Grindr
at 1:38am of a Wednesday.
The nearest Gay™ is 7 km away
and if I had to be brutally honest
like a hesitant carpenter, Norway somewhere,
wary of a wood-shortage in his perilous future,
I don't want the split-second warm
unpleasant-later feeling of his saliva
marking my dick like a dog against a tree.
I want to reach around
the green circle (online now!)
that lets me know they're the same as me:
awake, scrolling down like Croft
through a papyrus looking
for the right inscription.
And then our hands can reach,
join in the middle somewhere
across this pitch-black Donegal landscape,
and we wouldn't touch in the moonlight
as mystery insects buzz
by the fence posts, and ewes rest
under trees: content instead to watch new lambs
make their way through the darkness
to their mothers, in complete, holy silence.

Peter Wyton

FIRST DISOBEDIENCE

The consequence of sin
was first revealed to me
in Portadown, aged three,
because of indiscipline
on the road to Tandragee.

Astride my birthday trike,
longed for and highly prized,
I made an ill-advised
reconnoitre, infant-like,
completely unsupervised.

Adults were who knows where,
the garden gate swung back,
above, the sky turned black,
there was thunder in the air
as I left the cul-de-sac.

I circled, for a while,
the empty highway, then,
happy as Amundsen,
with my most complacent smile,
I set off for home again.

A boomerang of light
above my handlebars
shimmered like molten stars.
I was given a fearful fright
by Jesus, or Men from Mars.

Then a deluge ensued,
I scuttled back inside,
adamantly denied
misdemeanour to those rude
enough to enquire – and cried.

Why was I soaking wet?
Dripping, shivering, I
claimed to be wholly dry,
with irritated regret,
professed myself most upset.

And then our knocker knocked.
A very squelchy man
who drove the baker's van
maintained his way had been blocked,
by the trike held in his hand.

Yvonne Reddick

SPIKENARD

I trailed your flint and bayleaf scent to the porch,
but someone else's perfume was mixed with yours –

coiling with jonquils, spikenard, and something musky.
I paused at your alderwood door.

You were wreathed in the cologne I bought you:
Terre. Its heart-chord silex and bitter orange,

the base-note (which lingers longest) is Atlas cedar.
I remembered how I'd settle my cheek on your chest

to feel the stroke of your heart, until your fragrance
steeped my pores, and I'd breathe you in for weeks.

I pictured her hands at your belt, in that attic room –
my key still sprang the bolt.

Stephen Knight

IN MY OTHER LIFE

blue as the blue of who knows what
the sky fills every window of my other life
and the marble hallway is lit by sunbeams
angled unlike any I have known

down shaded streets where traffic seldom strays
streets on which the day has opened like a song
the walk towards a square I may not reach
is all I need of happiness

and all of this and you are there
in my other life and the children as children
where a table is laid where the xeremies drone
and we stop in a passage of light

how good I am in my other life
how willing to believe and how awake
awake to all the tiles and air and stones
of which my other life is built

here is the bakery here is the church
and this is where I catch the tram (the rattly tram)
now where do I have to be?
and who will meet me at the other end?

Notes on Contributors

Abayomi Animashaun is the author of two poetry collections, *The Giving of Pears* (2010) and *Sailing for Ithaca* (2014), both from Black Lawrence Press; and he is the editor of two anthologies, *Walking the Tightrope: Poetry and Prose by LGBTQ Writers from Africa* (Lethe Press, 2016), and *Others Will Enter the Gates: Immigrant Poets on Poetry, Influences, and Writing in America* (Black Lawrence Press, 2015).

Liam Aungier works as a civil servant in Dublin. He has had poems published in *The Irish Times*, *Cyphers*, and previously in *Poetry Ireland Review*. His first collection, *Apples in Winter*, was published by Doghouse Books.

Heidi Beck emigrated to the UK from America in 1998, and currently lives in the countryside near Bath. She holds MAs in English Literature (University of Chicago) and Creative Writing (Bath Spa University). Her poems have appeared or are upcoming in *Acumen*, *The Frogmore Papers*, *Poetry Salzburg Review*, and *Brittle Star*.

Fióna Bolger's work has appeared in *Southword*, *Brown Critique*, *Poetry Bus*, *The Chattahoochee Review*, and elsewhere. She has collections forthcoming with Yoda Press, Delhi (2019) and Salmon Poetry (2020). She is a co-ordinator of Dublin Writers' Forum, a member of Outlandish Theatre Platform, and is working towards a Ph.D. at DCU.

Maureen Boyle's debut poetry collection, *The Work of a Winter*, has just been published in its second edition by Arlen House. She is the inaugural recipient of the Ireland Chair of Poetry Travel Bursary. Her poem 'Strabane' will feature on BBC Radio 4's 'Conversations on a Bench' in January. She lives and teaches in Belfast.

Paul Bregazzi's poetry has appeared in *The Irish Times*, *The Stinging Fly*, *Magma*, and *Fields* magazine. His haiku and haibun feature in *The Shamrock Haiku Anthology II*, *Presence*, and *Contemporary Haibun Online*. He was selected for Poetry Ireland's Introductions series in 2015, and won the Cúirt New Writing Prize for Poetry, 2017. His first collection is forthcoming with Salmon Poetry.

Colette Bryce grew up in Derry and currently lives in Newcastle upon Tyne. Her latest collection, *The Whole & Rain-domed Universe* (Picador Poetry, 2014), received a Ewart-Biggs Award in memory of Seamus Heaney. Her *Selected Poems* (Picador Poetry, 2017) won the Pigott Poetry Prize at Listowel in 2018.

Jo Burns, born in Northern Ireland, now lives in Germany. Her publication credits include *Oxford Poetry*, *Southword*, *The Stinging Fly*, *The Tangerine*, and *Magma*. She won the 2017 McClure Poetry Prize (Irish Writers Festival, Los Gatos, CA) and the Magma Poetry Competition 2018. Her first collection, *White Horses*, has just been published by Turas Press.

Anthony Caleshu is the author of three books of poems (most recently, *The Victor Poems*, Shearsman 2015), and three books of criticism about contemporary poetry (most recently, editor of *In the Air: Essays on the Poetry of Peter Gizzi*, Wesleyan UP, 2018). He is Professor of Poetry at University of Plymouth, and founding editor of the small poetry press, *Periplum*.

Louise C Callaghan's collections, all with Salmon Poetry, are: *The Puzzle-Heart* (1999); *Remember the Birds* (2005); *In the Ninth House* (2011); and *Dreampaths of a Runaway* (2017). She edited an anthology of poetry called *Forgotten Light: Memory Poems* (A&A Farmar, 2003). In 2007 she was awarded an M.Litt. in Creative Writing from the University of St Andrews.

Lorraine Carey is from Donegal. Her poetry has been published in *The Honest Ulsterman*, *Prole*, *Atrium*, *Poethead*, *The Blue Nib*, and in several anthologies. In 2017 she was a runner-up in the Trócaire/Poetry Ireland Poetry Competition and *The Blue Nib* Chapbook Competition. Her first collection, *From Doll House Windows*, is published by Revival Press.

Rachel Coventry lives in Galway, where she is studying for a doctorate in philosophical poetics. Her poetry has appeared in *Poetry Ireland Review*, *THE SHOp*, *Cyphers*, and other outlets. Her debut collection, *Afternoon Drinking in the Jolly Butchers*, was published this year by Salmon Poetry.

Enda Coyle-Greene was born in Dublin. Her first collection, *Snow Negatives*, won the Patrick Kavanagh Award in 2006, and was published by Dedalus Press in 2007. Her most recent collection, *Map of the Last*, also from Dedalus Press, was published in 2013.

Greg Delanty's latest book in Ireland and Britain is *The Greek Anthology, Book XVII*, from Carcanet Press, which also published his *Collected Poems 1986-2006*. His latest book in the US is *Selected Delanty*, selected and introduced by Archie Burnett. His many awards include a Guggenheim for poetry. He works at Saint Michael's College, Vermont.

Mairéad Donnellan's work has appeared in various magazines and anthologies. Her awards include the Francis Ledwidge Poetry Award and the Trócaire/Poetry Ireland Poetry Competition. Her poetry has also been broadcast on RTÉ radio.

Michael Dooley's poems have appeared in *The Stinging Fly*, *Banshee*, *The Penny Dreadful*, and elsewhere. In 2018 he was featured in the anthology *The Best New British and Irish Poets* (Eyewear Publishing), and was shortlisted for the Cúirt New Writing Prize.

Terry Doyle's poetry has appeared most recently in *Crossways* and *The New Writer*. He is writing a first chapbook of poetry, and he works full-time in the Public Health Service in Cork.

John Fallon, born and bred in Dublin, lives with his wife in New York City, working as a freelance copywriter. His rites-of-passage novel, *A Relative Matter*, and his picaresque adventure, *A Peculiar Predicament*, are currently available. He is close to completing a first poetry collection, *Tick Tock*.

Orla Fay is the editor of *Boyne Berries*. Her work has appeared in *The Honest Ulsterman*, *Crossways*, *Lagan Online*, *Crannóg*, *The Bangor Literary Journal*, *Cyphers*, *Quarryman*, *The Pickled Body*, and *Skylight 47*. She is currently completing the MA in Digital Arts and Humanities at UCC.

Billy Fenton lives outside Waterford City, and he writes poetry and short stories. His work has been published in *The Irish Times*, and he was shortlisted for a Hennessy Award in 2018. He is currently completing a collection of stories.

Mary Finn, a Dubliner, is a novelist for children and young adults. (*No Stars at the Circus*; *Anila's Journey*; *The Horse Girl*; all published by Walker Books). She has worked as a teacher, a magazine journalist and a parliamentary reporter. 'On Samos', in this issue, is her first published poem.

Raine Geoghegan lives in West Sussex. She is half Romany with Welsh and Irish ancestry. Her poems and short prose have been widely published, and her debut pamphlet, *Apple Water: Povel Panni*, has just been published by Hedgehog Press.

Ruth Esther Gilmore is an American-born poet and composer. Her poetry has been published in English in the anthology *Moorgezeiten: Eine Anthologie* (Geest-Verlag, 2016). This year her poetry is also included in the Frankfurter Bibliothek Jahrbuch für das neue Gedicht: *Gedicht und Gesellschaft 2018*, *Auf der Flucht*, *Im Spiegel*, *Ein Segen* (Bretano-Gesellschaft Frankfurt/M.MBH).

John Greening's recent books include *To the War Poets* (Carcanet Press, 2013); *Heath* (Nine Arches Press, 2016) with Penelope Shuttle; and the anthologies, *Accompanied Voices: Poets on Composers* (Boydell and Brewer, 2015) and *Ten Poems about Sheds* (Candlestick Press, 2018). *The Silence* is due in 2019 from Carcanet Press. His awards include the Cholmondeley Award and the Bridport Prize, and he was recently resident artist at the Heinrich Böll Cottage, Achill.

Nicholas Grene is Emeritus Professor of English Literature at Trinity College Dublin, and a Member of the Royal Irish Academy. His books include *The Politics of Irish Drama* (Cambridge University Press, 1999), *Shakespeare's Serial History Plays* (Cambridge University Press, 2002), *Yeats's Poetic Codes* (Oxford University Press, 2008), *Home on the Stage* (Cambridge University Press, 2014), *Oxford Handbook of Modern Irish Theatre* (Oxford University Press, 2016) co-edited with Chris Morash, and *The Theatre of Tom Murphy: Playwright Adventurer* (Bloomsbury, 2017).

Maria Isakova-Bennett, from Liverpool, founded and creates the limited edition hand-stitched journal *Coast to Coast to Coast* (co-edited by Michael Brown). She was awarded a Northern Writers' Award in 2017, and is Artist and Poet in Residence at Poetry-in-Aldeburgh this year. Maria's pamphlet, *all of the spaces*, is published by Eyewear Publishing.

Mary Kathryn Jablonski, an artist and poet based in Saratoga Springs, New York, is the author of the chapbook *To the Husband I Have Not Yet Met*. Her poems and film/poem collaborations with Laura Frare have appeared in numerous print and online journals, including *Atticus Review*, *Beloit Poetry Journal*, *Poetry Film Live*, *Quarterly West*, *Salmagundi*, and *Tupelo Quarterly*.

Roisin Kelly – see page 113.

Lucia Kenny, born and raised in Larne, now lives with her husband in Silverdale, Lancashire, where she is a member of two creative writing groups. 'Roots', in this issue, is her first published poem.

Phil Kirby spent most of his working life teaching English. His first collection was *Watermarks*, from Arrowhead Press. His second collection, *The Third History*, from Lapwing Publications, appeared in 2018. Writing as PK Kirby, his novella for young adults, *Hidden Depths*, is available on Kindle.

Stephen Knight is the author of a novel and several collections of poems, most recently the pamphlet *A Swansea Love Song* (The Poetry Business, 2017).

Rosie Lavan is an Assistant Professor in the School of English at Trinity College Dublin. Her first book, *Seamus Heaney and Society*, will be published by Oxford University Press in 2019.

Ali Lewis was born in Nottingham. His poetry has appeared in *The Poetry Review*, *Ambit*, *The Rialto*, *Magma*, and elsewhere. He received an Eric Gregory Award in 2018.

Lottie Limb was born in Nottingham, and studied at Cambridge and Trinity College Dublin. Her M.Phil. in Irish Writing dissertation is entitled 'A Fool's Errand? Irish Ecocriticism and Reading Dermot Healy'. She writes essays and book reviews, and has published poems with the online arts collective *Big Birds*.

Christina Lloyd was born in Hong Kong and raised in Manila and San Francisco. Her work appears most recently in *The North*, and is forthcoming in *Epoch* and *The Frogmore Papers*. A doctoral candidate at Lancaster University, she is currently working on her first full-length collection.

Emer Lyons, originally from Cork, is a creative / critical Ph.D. candidate in the English department at the University of Otago, Dunedin. Her poetry and fiction have appeared in *Turbine*, *Mimicry*, *takahē*, *Southword*, *The Cardiff Review*, *London Grip*, *Queen Mob's Teahouse*, and elsewhere.

Kathleen McCann lives in Weymouth, MA, by the sea. In 2011 her full-length collection, *Barn Sour*, was a finalist for the May Swenson Poetry Book Award. She is looking for a home for her book-length manuscript, *Sail Away The Plenty*, poems written about Ireland and the famine years, beginning in 1845.

Mícheál McCann is a postgraduate student in the Seamus Heaney Centre for Poetry. His poems appear in *The Open Ear* and *Demand Change*. As dramaturg, he has adapted Anne Carson's *Nox* into a vocal chamber piece, and some of his poems are being set to music for the Derry International Choral Festival 2018.

Thomas McCarthy's most recent collection is *Pandemonium* (Carcanet Press, 2016). *Prophecy*, also from Carcanet Press, will be published in 2019.

Cecilia McGovern's *Polishing the Evidence* was published by Salmon Poetry. She is a former prizewinner at the Poetry Now festival in Dún Laoghaire, Co Dublin.

Medbh McGuckian's first collection, *The Flower Master*, was published by Oxford University Press in 1982. Since 1991, The Gallery Press has published 15 of her books. Her latest title is *Love, the Magician* (Arlen House, 2018).

Helen Meany is a journalist, critic, and arts consultant. She was the Arts Council's Literature Adviser from 2011-18. Previously she was Editor of *Irish Theatre Magazine*, curator of Critical Voices, and arts journalist and commissioning editor with *The Irish Times*.

Nancy Anne Miller is a Bermudian poet with seven collections, including: *Somersault* (Guernica Editions), *Immigrant's Autumn* (Aldrich Press), *Water Logged* (Aldrich Press), and *Star Map* (FutureCycle Press).

Deborah Moffatt was born in Vermont, and lives in Scotland. Her first collection was *Far From Home* (Lapwing Press, 2004). Two new collections will be published in 2019: *Eating Thistles* (Smokestack Books), and a collection in Gàidhlig. A dancer and musician, she at one time performed regularly at the Averof.

Jenny Carla Moran is a graduate of English Studies in Trinity College Dublin, and currently reads for her MA in Postcolonial Studies at SOAS, University of London. While in Trinity, she co-founded *nemesis*, the university's feminist journal. Her poetry has been published by *Icarus*, *Boshemia*, and *Unpredictapple*.

Marie Morrin is a native of Belfast, where she worked as a teacher of modern languages for ten years. Now settled in Dublin, she's working on a collection of poems. 'Godmother', in this issue, is her first published poem.

Annemarie Ní Churreáin is a poet from northwest Donegal. Her debut collection, *Bloodroot* (Doire Press, 2017), was shortlisted for the Shine / Strong Award for best first collection in Ireland, and for the 2018 Julie Suk Award in the USA. She is also the author of *Town* (The Salvage Press, 2018), a suite of poems about Dublin.

Niamh Nic Ghabhann is Assistant Dean, Research (Faculty of Arts, Humanities and Social Sciences) and Course Director, MA Festive Arts programme at the University of Limerick. Her monograph, *Medieval Ecclesiastical Buildings in Ireland, 1789-1915: Building on the Past*, was published by Four Courts Press in 2015.

John Noonan's work has appeared widely in journals, magazines, and anthologies. He is a former winner of the Goldsmith Poetry Award, and is currently working on a first collection.

Mary O'Donnell is a poet and fiction writer. Her interconnected story collection, *Empire*, was recently published by Arlen House. A chapbook of surrealist poems is due from SurVision Press. A member of Aosdána, she is currently a doctoral student at UCC.

Bernard O'Donoghue is Emeritus Fellow of Wadham College, Oxford, where he taught Medieval English and Modern Irish Poetry. His 2016 collection, *The Seasons of Cullen Church* (Faber and Faber), was shortlisted for the TS Eliot Prize.

Laurence O'Dwyer holds a Ph.D. in paradigms of memory formation from Trinity College Dublin. In 2018, he was a visiting scholar at the Scott Polar Research Institute at the University of Cambridge. He has received the Patrick Kavanagh Award for Poetry. His collection *Tractography* (Templar Poetry, 2018), received the Straid Collection Award.

Rugadh **Simon Ó Faoláin** i 1973 i mBaile Átha Cliath agus tógadh é in Iarthar Dhuibhneach. Tá trí leabhar filíochta Gaeilge foilsithe aige. I measc na ngradam atá buaite aige dá scríbhneoireacht tá Duais Glen Dimplex, Duais Strong, Duais Bhaitéar Uí Mhaicín, Duais Cholm Cille agus Duais Foras na Gaeilge. An leabhar is déanaí uaidh ná *An Corrmhíol*, aistriúchán Gaeilge ar an dán fada Gàidhlig *A' Mheanbhchuileag* le Fearghas MacFhionnlaigh.

Thomas O'Grady is a Prince Edward Island poet. His second book of poems, *Delivering the News*, will be published by McGill-Queen's University Press in 2019.

Colin Pink writes plays and poetry. *Acrobats of Sound*, a poetry collection, is available from Poetry Salzburg. His poems have appeared in magazines such as *Poetry News*, *THE SHOp*, *Poetry Salzburg Review*, *South Bank Poetry*, *Orbis*, and on-line in *Ink Sweat & Tears* and *The High Window*.

Justin Quinn's most recent collection is *Early House* (The Gallery Press, 2015). He lives in Prague.

Yvonne Reddick is the author of *Ted Hughes: Environmentalist and Ecopoet* and *Translating Mountains*. She has received a Northern Writer's Award, a Hawthornden Fellowship, a commendation in the 2018 National Poetry Competition, and The Peggy Poole Award. Her pamphlet *Spikenard* is a forthcoming Laureate's Choice. She lectures in Creative Writing and reviews for the *TLS*.

Nell Regan's third collection is *One Still Thing* (Enitharmon Press, 2014). Her awards include an Arts Council Literature Bursary, a Patrick and Katherine Kavanagh Fellowship, and a Fellow at the International Writing Programme, Iowa. Her biography *Helena Molony: A Radical Life* (Arlen House, 2017) was an *Irish Independent* Book of the Year.

Lex Runciman has published six collections of poems, including most recently *One Hour That Morning* in 2014, and *Salt Moons: Poems 1981-2016* in 2017, both from Salmon Poetry. Individual poems have been recognised with the Silcox Prize and the Kenneth O Hanson award. A chapter discussing his work concludes Erik Muller's critical book, *Durable Goods*. He lives in Portland, Oregon.

Elizabeth Scanlon is editor of *The American Poetry Review*. She is the author of *Lonesome Gnosis* (Horsethief Books, 2017), *The Brain Is Not the United States/The Brain Is the Ocean* (The Head & The Hand Press, 2016), and *Odd Regard* (Ixnay Press, 2013).

Kathryn Simmonds has published two poetry collections with Seren Books, *Sunday at the Skin Launderette* (2008) and *The Visitations* (2013). She lives in Norwich with her family, and is working on another book.

John Smelcer is the author of over 55 books, including a dozen books of poetry. For a quarter of a century, he was Poetry Editor at *Rosebud*.

Gerard Smyth has published nine collections of poetry, including, *The Yellow River*, with artwork by Seán McSweeney (Solstice Arts Centre, 2017), *A Song of Elsewhere* (Dedalus Press, 2015), and *The Fullness of Time: New and Selected Poems* (Dedalus Press, 2010). He is a member of Aosdána and Poetry Editor of *The Irish Times*.

Janet Sutherland has three collections with Shearsman Books, most recently *Bone Monkey*. Her poetry has appeared in anthologies and magazines such as *Poetry Review*, *New Humanist*, *The London Magazine*, *New Statesman*, and *The Spectator*. She received a 2018 Hawthornden Fellowship. Her fourth collection, *Home Farm*, is due in January 2019 from Shearsman Books.

Anne Tannam is a Dublin poet with two collections: *Tides Shifting Across My Sitting Room Floor* (Salmon Poetry, 2017), and *Take This Life* (WordOnTheStreet, 2011). A spoken word artist, Anne has performed at festivals and events in Ireland and abroad. She is co-founder of the weekly Dublin Writers' Forum, and regularly runs literary events across Dublin.

Mary Shine Thompson is a critic with a particular interest in contemporary poetry and the post-Yeats generation of poets.

Richard Tillinghast, who spent a number of years living in Co Galway and Co Tipperary, now divides his time between Hawaii and Tennessee. His most recent book is a nonfiction 'book of places', called *Journeys into the Mind of the World* (The University of Tennessee Press, 2017).

Jessica Traynor's debut, *Liffey Swim* (Dedalus Press, 2014), was shortlisted for the 2015 Strong/Shine Award. She is under commission from Poetry Ireland, the Association of Irish Choirs, and Chamber Choirs Ireland to create a choral piece with composer Elaine Agnew called 'An Island Sings', to be performed at the National Concert Hall in 2019. Her second collection, *The Quick*, has just been published by Dedalus Press.

Roderic Vincent is one of the Poetry Ireland Introductions poets for 2018. He came second and third in the Fish Poetry Prize, 2017. His poems are included in *The Iron Book of New Humorous Verse* (Iron Press), and in literary magazines including *Stand*, *The Rialto*, *Magma*, and *Prole*. He was shortlisted for The Poetry School/Nine Arches Press poetry Primers in 2015. He lives in Ludlow in Shropshire.

Christian Wethered features in the *The Best New British and Irish Poets 2018* (Eyewear Publishing), and he was shortlisted for the Melita Hume Prize (judged by Vahni Capildeo). His work was selected for the Poetry Ireland Introductions series, and he was third-placed in the Café Writers Competition (judged by Andrew McMillan).

Mary Wilkinson's writing features in *Crannóg*, 'An Irishwoman's Diary' in *The Irish Times*, *Books Ireland*, *West 47*, *The Dublin Quarterly*, *Tell Tale Souls*, and the *Listowel Writers' Week* anthology. She was shortlisted for Poems for Patience, 2013 and regularly contributes to RTÉ and Lyric FM.

Milena Williamson is from Swarthmore, Pennsylvania. Her poetry has been published by *The Tangerine*, *The Lifeboat*, *Resonance*, and the Poetry Jukebox in Belfast. She was the winner of the Mairtín Crawford Poetry Award in 2018, and is currently pursuing an MA in poetry at the Seamus Heaney Centre at Queen's University Belfast.

Peter Wyton's work features in *The New Oxford Book Of War Poetry*, and he has won many prizes in written poetry competitions and performance poetry slams. Proceeds from the sale of his work has raised money for Women's Aid, and he has been nominated twice for the Forward Prize.